Praise for

B.L.E.S.S.

"Inside each of us is a deep longing to make a difference, to leave our mark, to love the people around us in such a way that they see Jesus through us. *B.L.E.S.S.: 5 Everyday Ways to Love Your Neighbor and Change the World* takes that deep longing or desire and gives it legs—authentic and practical ways to actually do what you so want to do: love your neighbors and change the world."

–Mark Batterson, *New York Times* bestselling author of *The Circle Maker* and lead pastor of National Community Church

"Years ago, we were asking 'What would Jesus do?' In *B.L.E.S.S.: 5 Everyday Ways to Love Your Neighbor and Change the World*, Dave and Jon Ferguson show us not just what Jesus would do, but what Jesus did do. If every Jesus follower would simply seek to B.L.E.S.S. their neighbors using these biblical practices, we really could change the world again!"

–Andy Stanley, author, communicator, and founder of North Point Ministries

"Dave and Jon Ferguson's heart to reach people for Christ is truly inspiring. In their book *B.L.E.S.S.: 5 Everyday Ways to Love Your Neighbor and Change the World*, you will learn how to be an effective witness for Christ and how to love people where they are. If you have a heart to reach the lost, this book will motivate you and inspire you to make a difference with five simple ways to bless your neighbor with the love of Christ."

–Craig Groeschel, pastor of Life.Church and *New York Times* bestselling author

"Wow. I have literally been searching for a book like this. In *B.L.E.S.S.*, Dave and Jon Ferguson outline a profoundly simple, challenging-but-doable framework for loving your neighbors that isn't gimmicky, weird, or forced. These are also the kinds of practices that will resonate deeply with people in the post-modern, post-Christian era we're moving into. I love this book."
   —Carey Nieuwhof, leadership author and podcaster

"I have seen Dave and Jon's five B.L.E.S.S. missional practices implemented in hundreds of churches. Better than anything else I have ever experienced, these five simple practices release everyday people into powerful witness wherever they live, work, and play."
   —Dr. Rick Richardson, professor of evangelism and leadership at Wheaton College and the Wheaton College Billy Graham Center and author of *You Found Me*

"Dave and Jon Ferguson are experts at creating tools that inspire, equip, and empower people to live out their faith. This book is exactly that: equal parts motivation and practical application. It's not an academic theoretical thesis; we don't need any more eloquent ideas! We need exactly what this book offers: tried and true lived experience, honest and relevant practical plans that everyone can use every day to live the great adventure of faith. This book could easily be a handbook for every Christian leader to equip their people to live out their best hopes for a better world."
   —Danielle Strickland, spiritual leader, Kingdom entrepreneur, and ambassador of fun :-)

"Dave and Jon have an unusual knack—no, make that an unusual gift: to present important truths about the Gospel and how to live before God in our world in ways that are clear and memorable and doable. Jesus taught us to focus on loving God and loving others, and B.L.E.S.S. is all about loving God and learning over time to nurture a life that loves others: one prayer at a time, one conversation at a time, one meal at a time, one act of service at a time, and living into one story at a time. Each day we can live into B.L.E.S.S. one step at a time. Reading this book is a good first step."

—Reverend Canon Dr. Scot McKnight, professor of New Testament at Northern Seminary

"My friends Dave and Jon once again show us an important aspect of what it means to initiate and sustain movement. By embedding common practices that in turn embody the movement's DNA throughout the organization, the common practice of B.L.E.S.S. rhythms is their way of ensuring that NewThing Network always remains open to God and to people."

—Alan Hirsch, author of numerous books on missional spirituality and leadership and founder of 5Q Collective, Forge Missional Training Network, and more recently the Movement Leaders Collective

"The concept of loving our neighbor has never been more foreign to Christians and non-believers alike. We have fallen into a 'me and mine' mentality in which everything and everyone beyond ourselves aren't very high on our priority list. Yet Jesus told us to love our neighbor; He said it loud, clear, and often. With B.L.E.S.S., we're given the tools to put our love into action so that our neighbors see God through us. With so much unrest and uncertainty in the world, nothing is more welcome right now than a book on how to love as Christ loves."

—Albert Tate, co-founder and lead pastor of Fellowship Church

"*B.L.E.S.S.* is practical, powerful, and personal. This book will give you practical ways to love your neighbors, rely on the Spirit's power, and personally challenge you to join Jesus in His mission."
　　–Dr. Derwin L. Gray, lead pastor of Transformation Church and author of *The Good Life: What Jesus Teaches about Finding True Happiness*

"*B.L.E.S.S.* is an ingenious approach to evangelism that is tailor-made for today's world. Hundreds of churches and individuals are already engaging in the B.L.E.S.S. practices to reach the world for Jesus. I can't say it strongly enough: don't miss out on the B.L.E.S.S. movement!"
　　–Michelle T. Sanchez, executive minister of Make and Deepen Disciples for the Evangelical Covenant Church

"How many of us feel the pressure to share our faith yet are frustrated by the lack of significant and lasting results? Filled with key scriptural insights, helpful research, and practical everyday stories, *B.L.E.S.S.* will both encourage and equip you to love people well and see them respond authentically to Jesus. Whether you are new to the faith or have been walking with the Lord all your life, this is a book to absorb and pass along to others!"
　　–Kadi Cole, leadership consultant, executive coach, and author of *Developing Female Leaders* (www.kadicole.com)

"I believe the B.L.E.S.S. practices are simple enough for a child to understand. Simultaneously, they are robust enough to form ordinary folks into loving, fruitful missionaries who can plant the Gospel in new contexts and see new disciples made. The B.L.E.S.S. practices well-lived eventually lead to renewed communities that function like spiritual families around the person of Jesus. Dave and

Jon have given us the best handbook out there to make this practical and possible for all of God's people. I believe the future of the church rides on this loving missionary engagement being restored to the Church. This book is a needed and significant addition to that movement!"

—Rob Wegner, co-founder of Kansas City Underground, team leader for NewThing, catalyst for Disciples Made, and author of *The Starfish and the Spirit*

"I first heard about the B.L.E.S.S. practices from Dave and Jon Ferguson several years ago. For someone like me who wants to share the Gospel but doesn't consider themselves to be an evangelist, the practices have been transformative. When I first heard about B.L.E.S.S., I thought, 'I can do that!' And that's why I started sharing these same practices with the churches we serve. The Fergusons have given us a simple way to live out the Great Commission in our daily lives. This book will change how you—and your church—engage your mission."

—Tony Morgan, founder of the Unstuck Group and author of *The Unstuck Church*

"Never before have we needed clear, simple, and effective strategies to reach people with the love of Jesus more than we do now. I appreciate my friends Dave and Jon for articulating so well in this book a principle I have always believed: that when the Church takes practical, Gospel-centered action to reach people, we will change lives, communities, and nations for the Glory of God. This book will give you fresh language and new imagination for sharing a timeless Gospel in a changing world."

—Reverend James T. Meeks, senior pastor and founder of Salem Baptist Church of Chicago

"Dave and Jon Ferguson have inspired and trained many leaders across the world to follow Jesus and launch thriving churches. I am delighted they are sharing their wisdom and experience."
—Nicky Gumbel, vicar of HTB and pioneer of Alpha

"The genius of the lever is that it allows a small gesture of force to move a great weight. There is the same kind of genius in this book. Dave and Jon offer us a profoundly simple, accessible, and versatile approach to moving that great weight we feel when it comes to the work of evangelism and transformation. Hopeful and inspiring, their approach promises us joy instead of anxiety in the great work of both sharing and being good news to the people around us."
—Brian Sanders, founder of the Underground Network and author of *Microchurches: A Smaller Way*

"There is no simpler way to normalize the Great Commission and share the Gospel than B.L.E.S.S. I've found that it's the best way to get my church centered on Jesus and join God in the work that He is already doing in the lives of those they live, work, and play with."
—Daniel Im, pastor, podcaster, and author of several books, including *You Are What You Do: And Six Other Lies about Work, Life, and Love*

"At a time when our world desperately needs the Gospel, Dave and John Ferguson B.L.E.S.S. us with these five simple steps to love one another as of Jesus did, through everyday friendship and blessings."
—Joby Martin, lead pastor of the Church of Eleven22

"Dave and Jon Ferguson have always had a knack for creating strategic and practical processes that work in the real world. I still remember the first time they shared with me the simple steps behind the B.L.E.S.S. paradigm for missional relationships and evangelism. It struck me as both true to real life and within the reach of the average guy or gal. If you want to make a difference in your community and world, this is a book you need to read."

—Larry Osborne, author and pastor of North Coast Church

"I have known brothers Jon and Dave Ferguson for many years. They have consistently sought to mobilize the Church to reach out and help people make their way back to God. B.L.E.S.S is a simple yet powerful strategy to help the Church reach out to a hurting world at this critical time in history. More than ever the Church has the challenge and great opportunity to love people to Jesus outside its four walls."

—Mark Jobe, president of Moody Bible Institute

B.L.E.S.S.

B.L.E.S.S.

5 EVERYDAY WAYS TO LOVE YOUR NEIGHBOR AND CHANGE THE WORLD

DAVE FERGUSON AND JON FERGUSON

SALEM
BOOKS
an imprint of Regnery Publishing
Washington, D.C.

Scriptures marked CEV are taken from the CONTEMPORARY ENGLISH VERSION. Copyright © 1995 by the American Bible Society. Used by permission.

Scriptures marked EXB are taken from THE EXPANDED BIBLE. Copyright © 2011 by Thomas Nelson. Used by permission. All rights reserved.

Scriptures marked MSG are taken from THE MESSAGE. Copyright © 1993, 2002, 2018 by Eugene H. Peterson. Used by permission of NavPress. All rights reserved. Represented by Tyndale House Publishers, a Division of Tyndale House Ministries.

Scriptures marked NET are taken from THE NET BIBLE®, NEW ENGLISH TRANSLATION®.

Copyright © 1996 by Biblical Studies Press, LLC. All rights reserved.

Scriptures marked NIV are taken from THE HOLY BIBLE, NEW INTERNATIONAL VERSION®. Copyright © 1973, 1978, 1984, 2011 by Biblica, Inc.™ Used by permission of Zondervan.

Scriptures marked NKJV are taken from the NEW KING JAMES VERSION®. Copyright © 1982 by Thomas Nelson, Inc. Used by permission. All rights reserved.

Scriptures marked NLT are taken from THE HOLY BIBLE, NEW LIVING TRANSLATION®. Copyright © 1996, 2004, 2007, 2013, 2015 by Tyndale House Foundation. Used by permission of Tyndale House Publishers, Inc., Carol Stream, Illinois, 60188. All rights reserved.

Salem Books™ is a trademark of Salem Communications Holding Corporation
Regnery® is a registered trademark and its colophon is a trademark of Salem Communications Holding Corporation

ISBN: 978-1-68451-088-7
eISBN: 978-1-68451-104-4

Library of Congress Control Number: 2020945139

Published in the United States by
Salem Books
An Imprint of Regnery Publishing
A Division of Salem Media Group
Washington, D.C.
www.SalemBooks.com

Manufactured in the United States of America

10 9 8 7 6

Books are available in quantity for promotional or premium use. For information on discounts and terms, please visit our website: www.SalemBooks.com.

CONTENTS

Foreword

More than twenty years ago, I was already a follower of Jesus but was feeling lost when it came to what He wanted me to do with my life. I was a seminary graduate and had applied to be a pastor at several churches, but no one called me back. Someone suggested I think of planting a new church...because, *"Hey, if no church will hire you, maybe you should start one."*

I had never considered planting a church and had no idea where to begin. I heard about a church-planting conference and decided to check it out. I showed up and didn't know anyone. I spent the first thirty minutes standing off to the side, feeling self-conscious and awkward. When the first session started, I found a seat toward the back of the room. *I felt like the kid in elementary school sitting at the lunch table by himself.* That's when Dave Ferguson came up and introduced himself to me.

He said, "Hey, I'm here with the staff from my church, and you are welcome to sit with us. We're all gonna go grab a bite to eat after this, and we'd love to have you."

I spent the next few days hanging out with Dave and Jon and the rest of their team. They saw me, included me, and invited me to learn and eat with them. It would be hard for me to overstate the impact those days had on my life.

It would also be hard to overstate the impact Dave and Jon have had on the leadership of the Church today. With books and Bible studies, conferences and retreats, and certainly through their church in Chicago, they have informed and inspired us all with applicable action. That's what I love about *B.L.E.S.S.*

Some books you read for information, others for inspiration, and still others for application. What makes *B.L.E.S.S.* an exceptional book is that it has all three!

In the pages ahead, you will find information based on biblical truth, inspiration for how you can bring change to a world that desperately needs it, and clear application in the form of five practices for how to love your neighbor.

This book was written during a time when the world was tremendously divided and in search of answers—searching for a cure for a global pandemic, looking for remedies for systemic racism, and pursuing economic solutions for high unemployment. Even our pursuit of answers seems to pull us further to the left or to the right, and thus farther apart.

We know from the life of Jesus that love is the answer. But how do you practically love under these trying circumstances? *B.L.E.S.S.* is a book that will show you how to live out that love.

Dave and Jon Ferguson have provided thoughtful leadership in lots of areas—from planting a multisite missional church in Chicago (Community Christian Church) to launching a global church-planting movement (NewThing) and leading the charge of church multiplication through the Exponential Conference. But in my opinion, what they excel at most is creating simple, memorable, and reproducible practices for followers of Jesus. Because these practices are simple enough to understand, memorable enough to do, and shareable with others, they can be reproduced by anyone, anytime, anywhere.

That's why people all over the world are already using them. In this book, you'll read story after story of people finding and following Jesus because someone prayed for them, listened to them, ate with them, served them, and shared their story with them.

I hope that like me, you'll join Dave and Jon and begin to B.L.E.S.S. those around you. As you do, you will begin to see the people where you live, work, and play come to know the transforming love of God. And if enough of us will band together to do this, I agree with the Fergusons: *we can change the world!*

Are you with me?

Kyle Idleman
Senior pastor of Southeast Christian Church and author of
Not a Fan and *Don't Give Up*

Introduction

Last week a big orange moving truck pulled into the driveway next door, signaling that our new neighbors had just arrived. It's the house on your right as you face our home. Getting new neighbors is like the adult version of a new kid showing up at school. It's kind of exciting! They could become your best friends. They might turn out to be the smartest kids or best athletes in the class. On the other hand, this could be the last time you even notice them!

But no matter who my new neighbors turn out to be, the Bible's advice on how I am to treat them is clear. It says, *"Love your neighbor as yourself"* eight times. Not once. Not twice. Eight times! Loving your neighbor as yourself is so important to God that He not only repeats Himself, but also makes it a command. And it's not just one in a long list of many commands. Jesus coupled loving your neighbor along with the command to love God!

> Love the Lord your God with all your heart and all your soul and with all your mind and with all your strength. The second is this: Love your neighbor as yourself. There is no commandment greater than these. (Mark 12:30–31 EXB)

"Love your neighbor as yourself" is called the Royal Law. That sounds so beautiful. And it is—when we get it right.

But loving your neighbor isn't always easy. I once had next-door neighbors who constantly let their pit bull loose in my yard and then got busted for drug possession. They were hard to love. But most of my neighbors have been decent folks. So more often than not, the difficulty we face in loving our neighbors is because we simply don't know *how* to love them.

Maybe that is why God made it a command. He knew we'd struggle. He knew if He didn't make it a command, we'd treat it as optional. So God insisted that we find the time, make the sacrifice, and be intentional about loving our neighbors.

B.L.E.S.S.: 5 Everyday Ways to Love Your Neighbor and Change the World is a practical resource to help you obey God's command to love your neighbor. While this book is written in one voice (Dave's) to make it more readable, it comes from the experience, heart, and hard work of both Dave and Jon Ferguson. This book is written with a sincere desire to show you what the Bible, Jesus's life, contemporary research, and our own experiences have shown both of us about how to love your neighbors and show them the love of God. This is not a book written to merely change your thinking. It is written to change how you live your life. This book is a manual for how to intentionally and sacrificially make time to love your neighbors.

I'm excited that you are reading this book. As you learn the practices for loving your neighbors, many of them will come to love God and follow Jesus. It will change their lives. It will change their eternities! I'm convinced that if enough of us live out these everyday practices, we could actually change the world!

Let me explain the contents of this book so you can discover *how* to love your neighbor and learn what your part is in changing the world.

Who Is Your "Neighbor"?

Yes, your neighbor is the person who lives in the house or the apartment next to you or down the street. But just like Jesus defined *neighbor* more broadly in the story of the Good Samaritan (Luke 10:25–37), I will do the same. I will ask you to identify eight neighbors—people God has placed around you where you live, work, and play.

5 Everyday B.L.E.S.S. Practices

The five B.L.E.S.S. practices are the everyday ways that you are to love your neighbor and change the world. You will discover that these practices are grounded in the Old Testament but lived out by Jesus. They are:

- B: **B**egin with Prayer
- L: **L**isten
- E: **E**at
- S: **S**erve
- S: **S**tory

I will dedicate a whole chapter to each of these practices so that you both understand them and know how to live them out with your neighbors.

5 Simple B.L.E.S.S. Tools

To go along with the five B.L.E.S.S. practices, I will give you a simple tool for each. The tool with each practice is something that you can use immediately to love your neighbor. They are:

Simple Tool to **B**egin with Prayer: "Who Is My Neighbor?" Map
Simple Tool to **L**isten: Listening Questions
Simple Tool for **E**ating: Meal Calendar
Simple Tool for **S**erving: R-P-M-S
Simple Tool for **S**torytelling: Three-Part Story

B.L.E.S.S. Stories

Make sure you read the B.L.E.S.S. stories that are scattered throughout the book. These are either my own or stories told to me by people just like you who have used the five B.L.E.S.S. practices to love the people God has placed in their lives. These stories will inspire you and help you envision yourself using these five B.L.E.S.S. practices with your neighbors.

B.L.E.S.S. Basics

The B.L.E.S.S. Basics are an added bonus to make sure you know *how* to love your neighbors. There are a couple of these in every chapter; they are brief tips and short insights on how to make the most of these everyday ways to love your neighbor. I strongly encourage you to pause while reading each of them to help you better apply what you are learning to your life.

B.L.E.S.S. Discussion Questions

At the end of each chapter are B.L.E.S.S. Questions you can use to put into practice all you are learning with a small group or a team. You will use these B.L.E.S.S. practices more consistently when you are a part of a community of people who are all committed to them. If given the opportunity to read this book with others, please take it and use the discussion guide to go deeper. If you are not a part of a group, then use the B.L.E.S.S. Discussion Guide as a way to pause, reflect, and apply what you have personally learned after each chapter.

B.L.E.S.S. Pledge

Toward the end of the book is a B.L.E.S.S. Pledge that is designed to call you to a commitment. You will be asked to sign it as a promise that you will love your neighbors by using the B.L.E.S.S. practices. You will also have two other people sign it who will hold you accountable for this commitment. The hope is that you will not just read this book, but will live it out…every day!

After we spotted the big orange moving truck, my wife, Sue, and I went over and knocked on our new neighbors' door. They came out, and we introduced ourselves to each other. They were a young couple with a three-year-old and another baby on the way. She was excited about the schools in our community, and he talked about plans he had for the lawn.

There was no pit bull loose in the yard. No sign of a drug bust. But even if there had been, I was commanded to love them. So the next day, I began to pray for them…

CHAPTER 1

Why Does Sharing the Good News Feel So Bad?

BIG IDEA
Sharing the good news can be as
simple as being a good friend.

How could sharing "good news" always end up feeling so bad?
I couldn't figure out the answer. Like you, my life was changed by the love of God and the life of Jesus. And like you, I wanted to obey Jesus's command to "love your neighbor" and do my part to change the world. Also like you, I wanted my family, friends, and neighbors to experience the love of God.

So I tried loving them by sharing the good news with my words: a verbal witness. That resulted in a series of disasters!

Then I tried a completely different approach. I would share the good news simply by how I lived my life. The result of that seemed to be...well, nothing!

It seemed that however I tried to love others—with my words or through my life—it left either them or me feeling badly. What was I doing wrong? Where was the "good news" in all of this?

All that frustration led me to search for a simple way to share the love of God with those I cared about. Surprisingly (to me), that search

B.L.E.S.S. will make your life better!

The B.L.E.S.S. practices were created as a simple tool to help you bring the love of God to others. Your motivation is to help them know Jesus and experience eternal life, but people are often surprised to find that these practices make their own lives better too! You will discover that a life of praying, listening, sharing meals, serving, and telling stories is the richest life possible. The everyday rhythm of these five practices will not only change others and change you, but also begin to change your whole neighborhood. Those who commit to living out these practices will see the culture around them slowly shift from being just a group of people living in close proximity to each other to a neighborhood of people living in genuine community.

led me back to the Bible and how Jesus did it. I'm still shocked that I missed it for so long. Jesus had a simple, everyday way of sharing the good news that helped His "neighbors" come to know the love of God.

But I'm getting ahead of myself. Maybe if I start by telling you what didn't work for me, I can spare you some grief and disappointment.

Loving Others with Just My Words

I was baptized as a Christian at the age of ten, but I really became a Christ-follower late in my teens. And when I said "yes" to Jesus, it was the real deal! I experienced the unconditional grace of God, the hope of Heaven, and newfound purpose for my life. Along with that came a passion to share it all with others. As a young believer I looked for every opportunity to share my faith and my story.

Motivated by the Great Commission to "Go and make disciples" (Matthew 28:19 NIV), I tried street evangelism and—as one does in street evangelism—walked up to complete strangers, attempting to engage them in spiritual conversations. Each time, I would get *that look*. (You know that look—the one we always give crazy people.) Fail!

I was challenged by 1 Peter 3:15 to "always be prepared to give an answer to everyone who asks you to give the reason for the hope that you have" (NIV). So I got trained in how to share my testimony with non-believers. I decided it was a good idea to canvass my neighborhood and tell my story. Almost every time I knocked on the doors of people I didn't know, I got piercing stares from behind a screen and doors slammed in my face. Fail!

If Billy Graham Can Do It...

When I was in college, I was so passionate about sharing the good news of Jesus with others that I would have actual dreams about it. In those dreams, I would clearly articulate the grace of God, and my friends and loved ones would respond with knowing nods and convicted hearts. And each time before I woke up, my friends had said "yes" to Jesus and asked me to baptize them!

Only in my dreams.

In real life, my roommate Scott and I had just received scholarships to the Billy Graham School of Missions, Evangelism, and Ministry. What better organization than the Billy Graham Evangelistic Association to train us how to share our faith? Receiving a scholarship meant I would get an all-expenses-paid trip to Oklahoma City, where they were hosting crusades at night and training during the day. (I know, not exactly Newport Beach or New York City. But I was a college kid, and they were paying!) On top of that, we also would get excused from three days of classes! So we were all in.

Three days later, Scott and I were on our way back to college totally fired up, ready to change the world. As we drove back on Interstate 44, we were already planning how to apply everything we'd learned. We were eastbound in my rusted-out, cocoa-brown Toyota Corona when we saw a hitchhiker. I told Scott, "Let's pull over and give him a ride." With the two of us in the front seat and our new victim—I mean, "friend"—in the back, we introduced ourselves. We learned our new traveling companion was George.

For the next six hours, we peppered George with everything we had learned over the previous seventy-two hours. George was the first person we had met who was far from God since we were trained by the greatest evangelistic crusade organization in history. By the time we got back to school, George had confided in us that he didn't have a job or a home, but he did want to say "yes" to Jesus.

We were so excited that we called a local pastor, who opened his church and let us baptize George that same day! This was just like in the New Testament!

Now George needed a place to stay and help getting back on his feet. We convinced our resident assistant to let George stay in our dorm, and we got him a one-week meal pass. Scott and I were celebrating this new convert.

Until—(I think you can see where this is going)—two days later when George stole $150 from my roommate, hijacked another friend's car, and left town, never to be heard from again.

That was not exactly how it was supposed to work. I bet that never happened to Billy Graham or Cliff Barrows!

But undeterred by George, who in the space of forty-eight hours converted from Christ-follower to car thief, I continued to try every way possible to share the good news with others by using the Four Spiritual Laws, the bridge illustration, Evangelism Explosion, and spiritual conversation starters. I even started something I called the

---

You can't convert anyone.

If you're hoping to use the B.L.E.S.S. practices to convert someone, I have some bad news for you. Someone else already has that job, and it isn't you! It's the job of the Holy Spirit to convict and to convert (John 16:8-11). It's good that your desires are aligned with God's; He "desires all men to be saved and to come to the knowledge of the truth" (1 Timothy 2:4). But you can't convert your family member, friend, or coworker. So if you are feeling pressure to say or do something "right" so someone else can find and follow Jesus, the pressure is off! Only the Holy Spirit can do that! Relax and realize that is not your role. But you can join Him in His work and bless the people around you. Just do the blessing and let God do the converting!

"Soul Winners Club." (Too embarrassing to explain.) In short, I tried everything!

Each of those methods was either too complicated, too time-consuming, or just plain relationally awkward. No matter how hard I tried to share my faith, it always turned out to be a "fail!" It just didn't make sense to me that talking about such good news should always end up feeling so bad!

Loving Others with Just My Life

There had to be a better way to love my neighbor than insisting they hear good news whether they wanted to or not. I was ready to make a complete shift and no longer verbally assault others with my Gospel story. From now on I would love my neighbor through how I lived my life. The words of Saint Francis of Assisi—"Preach the Gospel at all times, and if necessary use words"—captured my imagination. Or at the very least, those words gave me permission not to accost strangers with the Gospel.

For the next several years, I focused on living like Jesus and just waited for people to come to me with their spiritual questions. I did get a few—and I would help those people. But the only reason that happened was because I was a pastor at the church my brother, Jon, and I had planted. It was my job to live like Jesus and answer spiritual questions.

The church we started grew large, spreading to multiple locations. We saw lots of people discover the love of God and follow Jesus during that time. But what I seldom saw were people in my neighborhood—people I saw every day—coming to know the love of God and following Jesus. I seldom had spiritual conversations with the people who lived where I lived or played where my family and I played.

I knew that something was definitely wrong with that, and I made two discoveries. First, Saint Francis probably never said, "Preach the Gospel at all times, and if necessary use words." Second—and more importantly—I discovered that while I pastored a church with thousands, I had almost no spiritual influence in my neighborhood.

We Are All Frustrated!

The frustration of trying to love people, share the truth, and shoulder the weight of feeling badly was debilitating. But I was not alone. To my surprise, I discovered that lots of people feel that way.

And maybe you feel that way too. You probably haven't made as many awkward approaches as I did. But the more I researched it, the more I discovered that lots of us are frustrated and confused about how to love people in a way that includes sharing the good news of a loving God.

We want to be a light in a dark world, and we want others to experience what we have experienced—but we are so discouraged that we are on the verge of completely giving up on that conviction.

However, we are not the only ones who are frustrated. Our neighbors and friends are equally frustrated with *how* we love them and *how* we talk about the spiritual part of our lives! You might be surprised to learn they are absolutely interested in spirituality—but not in the way we are presenting it to them. Or because of our passivity, they have no idea we have a faith at all! Our neighbors are also confused and frustrated.

Let me give you a quick summary of the latest research that validates why all of us are frustrated.

Confused Christians

Surveys show that as believers, we are really confused about sharing our faith. When practicing Christians were presented with the statement "Part of my faith means being a witness for Jesus," 96 percent said that they "strongly agreed" or "somewhat agreed."[1] This was a consistent response across all age groups. When practicing Christians were asked if they agreed with the statement "The best thing that could ever happen to someone is for them to come to know Jesus," 96 percent agreed. However, 28 percent also believed that "it is wrong to share one's personal beliefs with someone of a different faith in hopes that they will one day share the same faith"[2]—and that percentage jumped to 46 with practicing Christians in their twenties and thirties.

Huh? How does that make sense?

It doesn't! But maybe that's the point. The data demonstrate just how confused and frustrated believers are about sharing the good news of Jesus! The inner conversation on this topic for many might go something like this: *My faith has made a huge difference for me, and I know it could help others…Jesus tells us it's good news, and I should share it…But whenever I try to present the Gospel, I feel like I'm selling a used car or I'm part of a pyramid scheme!…So maybe what I'm hearing from society—that "evangelism is wrong"—is actually right…Perhaps I shouldn't even try doing this!* Ever find yourself thinking along these lines?

Non-Christians Know What They Want

According to Gallup, 87 percent of Americans say they believe in God.[3] How significant is that? Think about your ten closest friends and neighbors. This stat indicates that on average, eight or nine of them believe there is a God. I'm not suggesting they are religious or that they are churchgoers. They probably aren't. I'm also not so naïve as to think that believing in a god means they have a relationship with Jesus. Most do not! The point is that most of the people around you already believe in a god, and they just need someone they trust to help them find their way back to the One True God. Discovering the best way to do that is why I wrote this book and why it will be helpful to you.

Before I get to the how-tos, here is some more good news: More than one in four non-Christians would say they are curious about Christianity and what it could mean for their lives.[4] And when you present this question to young adults in their twenties and thirties, the percentage of those who are curious about Jesus and faith jumps from 26 percent to 36 percent. This is great news! Not only do the vast majority of your friends and neighbors believe in God, but somewhere between one-fourth and one-third are currently searching and interested to learn more about Jesus.

And here is the kicker: 79 percent of unchurched people[5] agreed with the following statement: "I don't mind talking to a friend about their faith if they really value it." So within friendship, the vast majority of people are willing to talk about spiritual things.

So where do we go from here? Great question!

What Your Neighbors Want Most

In an eye-opening study, Barna Group[6] asked your friends and neighbors what they value in a person with whom they would talk about spiritual matters. Here are the top three qualities, in order.

1. **Listen without judgment.** Listening is one of the purest acts of love! What our neighbors want is for someone to lean in and just listen. They want someone who will assume the best. They desire to have another person absorb their questions and stories—not so you can come to a verdict, but so they can process their feelings and experiences in relationship.

The sad news is that two-thirds of the people surveyed said they had no one in their life who would listen to them without judgment. None. This reflects the sad truth that Christians are known more for talking than listening.

As I reflect on many of my attempts to share the good news, the focus was always about what I would say. I did most of the talking. And if I did ask a question, it was not so I could actually listen, but so I could maneuver the conversation to give me a chance to respond with my answers. My intentions were good, but in retrospect I often did way too much talking, and I prejudged what other people needed.

Here is some very encouraging news based on the research: Listening without judgment is something we are all capable of doing. It's love. It's grace. It's being a real friend.

2. **Allow them to draw their own conclusions.** Your friends and neighbors are not projects; they are people.

They are looking for someone who will "not force a
conclusion" on them but will trust them to have their
own spiritual journey.

When I think about my failed attempts, I think my heart was in a
good place, but my strategies were awful. If I was approaching a stranger
on the street or using a canned approach to the Gospel with a friend, I
knew the outcome I wanted. I wanted them to say "yes" to Jesus. Good
intention; poor tactic.

This is where both God and our friends want us to get out of the
way. If the Gospel is true and someone is sincerely searching for truth,
it will prove itself. We need to trust God to do His part and trust those
around us to journey just like we did.

Our friends want us to love, listen, and interact with them, but let
God draw them in. Jesus didn't coerce or trick people into saying "yes"
or a sinner's prayer. He trusted them, and He loved them (much more
on this later). Be a friend to your neighbors and trust God to do the rest.

3. **Confidence in sharing your own perspective.** After you
   have listened to your friend—once you have given them
   space to come to their own conclusions—it's then and
   only then that the people around us are interested in our
   confidently "sharing our own perspective." They want
   to know our stories and hear our experiences. But they
   also want to know that it is real, genuine, and that we're
   coming from a place of confident conviction.

I call it "paying the relational rent." Once you have invested enough
in the relationship by listening to them and loving them no matter what
they ultimately decide, you will have a permanent place in their life.
You'll be able to speak with confidence about the difference the love of
God and the life of Jesus have made for you.

Earning the right to tell your story and not just waylay someone with truth is very important. When we delve deeper into the research, we see that when our friends are presented with the open-ended statement *"I'd be more interested in learning about Christianity if...",* they complete it by saying:

"...*if Christianity had better evidence to support it."*

or "...*if I had an eye-opening spiritual experience myself."*[7]

Your story is the best evidence you can offer anyone! Your story cannot be irrelevant. If you have a strong relationship with the person you're sharing with, your story will be seen as empirical evidence. You cannot have an "eye-opening spiritual experience" for them, but you can share the difference the grace of God has made in your past, present, and future!

People Are Looking for Friends!

If I had to summarize what the research and my experience told me about what those around us are looking for, I could do it in one word: friend!

The research confirms it. What else would you call someone who listens without judgment, offers you wise counsel but helps you make your own decision, and loves you no matter what? That's a friend!

Friend /frend/ (noun)—a person whom one knows and with whom one has a bond of mutual affection....[8]

It's that simple. It's also that challenging. People are looking for you to be a friend. They are looking for a friend who will live the good news, be good news, and then share the good news in the form of their own story. In that order! Wow! It was that simple "Aha!" that brought me back to the Bible and opened my eyes to see that this is exactly how Jesus did it.

"Friend of Sinners"

Do you know what Jesus's nickname was? It was "Friend" (Matthew 11:16–19 NIV). More specifically, "Friend of Sinners."

Who gave Jesus that nickname? Religious leaders who watched how He lived His life and didn't like it. But apparently Jesus liked it so much that He kept it!

It was easy for "Friend of Sinners" to stick because everywhere Jesus went, He befriended people and was a blessing to them. His entire life and ministry were a rhythm of befriending and blessing. Jesus blessed every person and every place He encountered.

For example, He met two brothers, Peter and Andrew, a couple of working-class fishermen. For the next three years, they were the best of friends, and Jesus blessed them by teaching them, showing them miracles, and giving them a mission for their lives. In a much briefer encounter, Jesus shocked Zacchaeus, the chief tax collector, with His offer of friendship. The two shared the blessing of a meal and conversation, and Zacchaeus left a changed man.

In fact, as word spread far and wide about how Jesus blessed people, one of His friends, Mark, described what happened: "*People were bringing children to Jesus so that he would...bless them.... Then he hugged the children and blessed them*" (Mark 10:13, 16 CEV). Jesus proved that when you are a good friend who blesses people, you don't have to sell them anything or trick them into doing anything. Instead, they come to you!

Jesus's mission was to "*seek and save the lost*" (Luke 19:10 NIV), but His simple strategy was friendship and blessing.

The more I look at Jesus, the more I realize how I got it so wrong:

I made the good news complicated when it should have simply come from my heart.

I tried to manipulate something that was meant to fit into everyday life.

I made something relationally awkward that was meant to be a blessing stemming from friendship.

And I tried to make something happen that only God could do.

And there were times when I was passive while God was at work.

A rhythm of friendship and blessing was how Jesus loved people and proclaimed the good news. *Could that work for me? Could that work for the people in my church? Could I have overlooked something so very obvious and simple?* The more questions I asked, the greater my conviction grew that it could definitely work for me and for you.

A Simple, Everyday Way

So here is how I would like to help you in the following pages of this book…

I want to help you understand how to love your neighbor the way that Jesus did.

I want to help you avoid making the good news complicated when it should simply come from your heart.

I also want to spare you from relationally awkward conversations, because the Gospel was meant to be shared in routine exchanges between friends and neighbors.

I want to give you five simple ways you can bless people within the rhythm of everyday life!

Lastly, I want to make sure that you understand what God's responsibility is and what your responsibility is. I don't want you to try to be God or for you to expect God to do something He's asked *you* to do.

I believe wholeheartedly that very soon the people you love and the neighbors who live around you will come to know the love of God and follow Jesus because you have been a blessing to them.

It's really that simple. I promise!

In the next chapter, I'll tell you how an email from a stranger confirmed all this for me. It convinced me that this simple rhythm of friendship and blessing was not only Jesus's strategy for loving others and changing the world, but was actually God's plan—from the first pages of Genesis.

B.L.E.S.S. Discussion Questions

OPEN: How did you first learn about the love of Jesus and choose to follow Him?

_____

_____

_____

_____

_____

_____

DIG: What is your greatest fear or frustration when it comes to loving people and sharing the good news of Jesus with those around you?

_____

_____

_____

_____

_____

Read Matthew 28:19, Acts 1:8, and 1 Peter 3:15. What is your gut-level, first reaction to these scriptures? In what ways are you motivated or demotivated by these scriptures?

_____

_____

_____

_____

_____

What are you hoping to learn or gain from reading this book?

_____

_____

_____

_____

Think about the three qualities people said they want in someone with whom they would discuss spiritual matters. How well do you exhibit these qualities to your friends and neighbors who don't know Jesus? What steps can you take to grow in these areas?

_____

_____

_____

_____

Jesus's nickname was "friend of sinners" (Matthew 11:16–19 NIV). What changes might you need to make in order to be known as a friend of sinners?

_____

_____

_____

_____

_____

REFLECT: Who are some of the people around you that you would love to impact with the love of Jesus?

_____

_____

_____

_____

Pray for the people you hope to B.L.E.S.S.

_____

_____

_____

_____

_____

CHAPTER 2

Could Simply B.L.E.S.S.ing People Really Work?

BIG IDEA
God's plan for loving your neighbor and changing the world is through B.L.E.S.S.ing.

"**B**lessers versus Converters"

That was what the subject line in the email said. I didn't know who had sent it, but as I read the contents, I could see why he was so excited about his doctoral dissertation. (This might be the first time I've ever used the terms "excitement" and "doctoral dissertation" in the same sentence.)

The sender shared a single chapter titled "Blessers versus Converters" that cited research based on two teams of missionaries who went to Thailand. While both teams went with similar goals, they carried two distinctly different strategies.

The "Converters" group went with the sole intention of converting people and evangelizing. Their goal was to "save souls."

The "Blessers" group explained their intention like this: "We are here to bless whoever God sends our way."

The study followed both the "Converters" and the "Blessers" for two years. At the end of that time, the researchers discovered two key findings:

First, the presence of the "Blessers" in the community resulted in tremendous amounts of "social good." It appeared, according to the

Pick your primary context.

Where will you live out the B.L.E.S.S. practices? In your neighborhood? Or does it make more sense for you to practice them at your place of employment? Or maybe you will decide to apply these rhythms where you play, where you know people best? If you are tempted to say "All of the above," that is not a correct answer. There are two ways to keep the B.L.E.S.S. practices from being effective: the first is not doing them, and the second is trying to do them in too many places! Even the most well-intentioned people will not be able to go deep enough relationally with three or four different networks of people. If you want to see the transformational impact of these simple, everyday ways of loving your neighbor work, just pick one primary context.

study, that this group contributed to the betterment of society, community life, and the creation of social capital. The presence of the "Converters," however, seemed to make no difference.

The second discovery—and this was very surprising—was that the "Blessers" saw forty-eight conversions while the "Converters" saw only one! The "Blessers" group saw almost fifty times as many conversions through being a blessing than the group that was only trying to convert the people around it.

The bottom line: the best way to accomplish Jesus's mission of helping people love each other and come to know the love of God is for His people to become "Blessers!"

The B.L.E.S.S.ing Strategy

I shared the study with my brother, Jon, and we were so compelled by this information that we both started to research

Scripture to discover more about this "B.L.E.S.S.ing" strategy. Somehow, I had always thought that God's mission started when Jesus came to Earth, or when He commissioned His closest followers to "go and make disciples." The truth is that our God is a missionary God, and He had a mission for His people way back in the very beginning—in Genesis.

Take a look at what God said to Abram:

> *The Lord had said to Abram, "Go from your country, your*
> *people and your father's household to the land I will show*
> *you.*
> *I will make you into a great nation,*
> *and I will bless you;*
> *I will make your name great,*
> *and you will be a blessing.*
> *I will bless those who bless you,*
> *and whoever curses you I will curse;*
> *and all peoples on earth*
> *will be blessed through you." (*Genesis 12:1–3 NIV)

One word is repeated five times in just three short verses. Do you see it? God says to Abram, "I will bless you…and you will be a blessing…and I will bless those who bless you…and not only that…all people on earth will be blessed through you." Wow! There it is right in Genesis 12. God's very first strategy for reaching the world was "blessing."

The backstory on all this is that Abram's future was very much in doubt. He and Sarai (as they were then known) did not have a son yet to carry on his legacy. You might say that the mission of human beings had come to a screeching halt, which interestingly enough is often the place where the mission of God can finally take off—when we realize that our own efforts are not getting the job done. We look around and

B.L.E.S.S. is not a checklist.

Many well-intentioned people have taken these missional rhythms and turned them into a set of linear steps to be performed one at a time. Wrong! The B.L.E.S.S. practices are not a checklist or another church program you graduate from, nor a class where you earn a certificate. They are simple, everyday ways to bless the people around you. Warning! If you treat them like a checklist, your neighbors will feel like a project, and you will push them away from both you and God. Never focus more on the practices than on the people you are seeking to bless!

see a world in shambles. And it's in that place of desperation that the mission of God will often finally flourish.

And so God said to Abram, "Go." In Matthew 28, Jesus repeats God's words by telling His disciples, "Go into all the world...." Our God is constantly on the move, and He wants His people to be on the move as well. It's His desire that wherever we go—as we go—we are about the mission of befriending and blessing the people we come across. That is how we love each other and show the love of God.

Not only are we to be on mission wherever we go and as we go, but everything we need to accomplish that mission comes from God. And God says, "I will bless you, and then you will bless others with that very blessing. I'm not blessing you so you can hoard it or just reflect on how good it feels to be blessed." No, God says we are "blessed to be a blessing." He is saying to us, "However I have blessed you, use that to bless others. You don't have to manufacture anything—just bless others with who you are and all that I have given you."

Jesus's B.L.E.S.S.ing Strategy

There is no better model for what it looks like to "go and bless" than Jesus. His entire life was a blessing. The Gospels give us numerous examples of how Jesus blessed the people He encountered.

He also taught others how they could be blessings and receive God's blessing. In His most famous teaching, the Sermon on the Mount, He began with what is known as the Beatitudes and gave nine ways you could live a "blessed" life.

From the time Jesus left Heaven, came to Earth, and went back again, there wasn't a single breath, not a single blink of His eyes, not a moment of time in which He wasn't used by God to bless the people He encountered.

Luke, a doctor and historian, recorded one of the most powerful examples of this from Jesus's life. Take a look at how this story starts out. It may seem like an insignificant detail, but don't miss it.

> Jesus entered Jericho and was passing through. A man was there by the name of Zacchaeus; he was a chief tax collector and was wealthy. He wanted to see who Jesus was, but because he was short he could not see over the crowd. So he ran ahead and climbed a sycamore-fig tree to see him, since Jesus was coming that way. (Luke 19:1–4 NIV)

Notice in that first line that Jesus was "passing through" Jericho. He was headed somewhere else. So spending time with Zacchaeus wasn't something He planned weeks in advance. It likely wasn't in His Google calendar. But the opportunity to bless Zacchaeus presented itself as Jesus was "passing through" and living life.

And what we could easily miss is that Jesus chose to stop and spend time with a man that most people hated. Zacchaeus was a tax collector. Tax collectors made their living by ripping people off! If you lived back then and you were in a 35 percent tax bracket, Zacchaeus would charge you 50 percent and then pocket 15 percent for himself! But even so, Jesus invited Himself to Zacchaeus's house for a meal which, in that day, was a clear act of friendship. And Jesus's act of blessing so moved Zacchaeus that this chief tax collector immediately promised to give away almost everything he owned. Zacchaeus found salvation. I love how Jesus put an exclamation point on their new friendship:

> Jesus said to him, "Today salvation has come to this house, because this man, too, is a son of Abraham. For the Son of Man came to seek and to save the lost." (Luke 19:9–10 NIV)

Think about the magnitude of this blessing. Zacchaeus, a tax collector who was despised by his own people as a traitor working for the Roman government, is now called "a son of Abraham." He is now "blessed to be a blessing." What was true of Abraham became true of Zacchaeus in that moment, and it is also true of us today.

You Are Blessed to Be a Blessing

Abraham was blessed to be a blessing.

Abraham's descendants were blessed to be blessings.

Jesus was blessed to be a blessing.

Zacchaeus was blessed to be a blessing.

And now, in Jesus, we receive that same blessing.

God's plan for loving our neighbors and changing our world is that same simple blessing strategy. Paul, in his letter to a church in Galatia, drew a straight line from Abraham to us:

B.L.E.S.S. in the city

Lawrence worked for a nonprofit on the North Side of Chicago, a couple miles from where Jon lives today. He was excited about the opportunity to reach the people in his neighborhood with the love of Jesus.

Lawrence said, "I knew we were called to live in the city. And while we lived there we wanted to be the hands and feet of Jesus to the people we encountered." Lawrence doesn't remember exactly where he came across the B.L.E.S.S. acronym, but he said, "This tool solidified for us the trajectory of what we felt the Holy Spirit was already telling us to do—to simply be Jesus in very practical ways to people around us."

Whenever he was around people, Lawrence would keep the B.L.E.S.S. practices in mind. On one occasion, he sat down at a bus stop next to Gerald, who was texting on his smartphone. "I whispered a quick prayer for him under my breath, and then we just started talking. We continued the conversation while we rode the bus together, and before Gerald got off the bus, we exchanged phone numbers. That was the beginning of our friendship."

One of the things about B.L.E.S.S. that Lawrence loved was how it helped him be much more intentional about reaching out to people and simply praying, listening, and sharing coffee or meals together. He said, "I also found that these practices helped me exchange phone numbers with lots of people while I lived on the North Side."

Lawrence continued to build a friendship with Gerald. Most of the time when they got together, it was in local cafés. On one occasion, they were in the middle of a conversation when Jon walked in. "I had met Jon before," Lawrence recalled, "but I just about fell off my chair as one of the very people who came up with these B.L.E.S.S. practices walked into the cafe while I was actually living them out." Lawrence, who had already explained the B.L.E.S.S. practices to Gerald, told him that one of the creators had just walked in. Lawrence reintroduced himself to Jon and said, "You're not going to believe this, but I am doing the 'E' in B.L.E.S.S. right now. I'm 'B.L.E.S.S.ing' my friend at that table over there."

That was the beginning of a growing friendship between Jon and Lawrence. Since then, they've gotten together from time to time to share life and discuss how they can better B.L.E.S.S. people in their community. Lawrence says, "If I didn't have access to the simplicity of that tool you guys developed for Christians like me, I'm not sure I would have ever built that meaningful friendship with Gerald and many other people in my neighborhood, and I doubt I would have ever gotten to know Jon."

Understand, then, that those who have faith (he is referring to us) are children of Abraham. Scripture foresaw that God would justify the Gentiles by faith, and announced the gospel in advance to Abraham: "All nations will be blessed through you." So those who rely on faith are blessed along with Abraham, the man of faith. (Galatians 3:7–9 NIV)

Check it out: The same promise of blessing for Abraham is a promise to us if we choose to follow Jesus. We are blessed! But here's what we can't miss: This blessing was never meant to be something we keep to ourselves. Jesus said that if we believe in Him, streams of living water will flow from within us (John 7:38). Our lives aren't meant to be buckets of blessing for us to hoard and hold on to. Blessing is meant to flow. We're not buckets; we're rivers!

#Blessed

Let's pause for a second and make sure we're keeping it real. Personally, I want a biblical, practical, real-life way to love my neighbors and share Jesus—and if you're reading this book, then you do too. A "blessing strategy" sounds good, but it feels kind of fuzzy and more like a hashtag than a strategy. *#Blessed.*

What Do I Do?

Your next questions might be the same as ours: *So what do I do now? How do I actually be a blessing in the life of my neighbor? Are there some guidelines for this B.L.E.S.S.ing strategy? What does it look like, and how can I intentionally be a blessing?*

With those questions driving both Jon and me, we took a look at the life of Jesus to see if there were any recurring patterns in how He befriended and blessed the people in His life. The more we combed through the Gospels, the more we began to see some simple practices He routinely employed.

We made a list of all those simple practices and narrowed it down to the top five we believed people can do on a regular basis. After we identified the top five, we focused on making them simple and unforgettable. We put them into a memorable acrostic: B.L.E.S.S. That's how we discovered the B.L.E.S.S. practices: five everyday ways that Jesus loved His neighbors.

B.L.E.S.S.

Let me briefly highlight the five B.L.E.S.S. practices here through Jesus's words and actions. Later, I'll go into more depth to explain how you can live them out. With each chapter, in addition to the B.L.E.S.S. practices, you'll get a simple tool you can use to implement these practices in your everyday life.

B: Begin with prayer

When Jesus started His earthly mission, Luke 6 tells us that *He went out on a mountain and prayed*. Prayer is both how you discover your mission and how you live out the mission. Over and over again, we see Jesus retreating to pray. If you're not sure who God is calling you to bless or where God is calling you to go to be a blessing, you can begin with prayer. And if you know the people you want to bless, begin praying for those people now.

L: Listen

Asking questions and then listening was central to Jesus's life and teachings. Consider the blind man in Luke 18. Jesus didn't assume the blind man wanted to see. First, He asked, "What do you want me to do?" Then He listened (more on this story later). In the Gospels, Jesus asked many more questions than He answered. Of the 183 different questions He received, Jesus answered only a handful. Any relationship starts with listening to someone's words and life. True listening may be the kindest and most loving gift you can give someone.

E: Eat

Jesus liked to eat! Over and over, as in Matthew 9, we find Jesus with tax collectors and sinners…doing what? Eating! There is something about sharing a meal together that moves any relationship past acquaintance toward friendship—faster than just about anything else we can do.

S: Serve

Jesus told us straight up, "The Son of Man did not come to be served, but to serve...." (Matthew 20:28 NIV). He modeled for us that once you begin with prayer, listen, and eat with someone, there is a good chance that you'll discover how you can best serve the person God is asking you to bless.

S: Story

When people were ready to listen, Jesus would share His story. Like when doubting Thomas came to him asking, "How can we know the way?" Jesus answered, "I am the way and the truth and the life. No one comes to the Father except through me" (John 14:5–6 NIV). When you befriend and bless people, they feel relationally safe and want to know your story. Then, and only then, you can tell them how the love of God and Jesus's life, death, and resurrection have changed you.

Could B.L.E.S.S. Really Work?

Would it really work? That question continued to echo in my mind. I still was not convinced that God could use these five simple practices to change the life of a friend or neighbor. It's kind of embarrassing to admit that, especially because it's God who gave the B.L.E.S.S.ing strategy to Abraham, then saw it lived out in the life of Jesus and proclaimed by Paul as something for everyone who has "faith." Those are some heavy hitters! Their truth should be our truth.

Maybe my hesitance to fully buy in was because I had tried so many other approaches that failed. Maybe it was because Jon and I were considering teaching these to several thousand people in our church. Or maybe it was a combination of doubts that caused me to keep wondering, *Would these simple, everyday ways change the life of my neighbor?*

There was only one way to find out. I started using the five B.L.E.S.S. practices myself. I decided I would experiment and make two commitments:

1. I would use one B.L.E.S.S. practice every day.
2. I asked my small group to ask me, "Who did you B.L.E.S.S. this week?"

The following story is about one of the first people I tried to befriend and B.L.E.S.S. See if you can identify the five practices.

Experiment: B.L.E.S.S.ing My Friend

Every day, I wrote "B.L.E.S.S." in my journal and then underneath it a short list of people to pray for and maybe get to know better. One of those was my friend Michael. We became friends because our sons ran cross-country on the same high school team, and we both loved the sport. Michael was the kind of guy who would never walk into a church on his own. Not because he hated the church or had something against it; it just never would have occurred to him. I asked him about church once, and as kindly as he could, he said, "It just seems like bullshit!"

I knew him as a self-made man. He overcame an abusive home life as a kid by moving out on his own as a teenager. He went on to become a successful college athlete, marry a beautiful woman, start his own company, and enjoy all the benefits of success.

But Michael had a secret. He had been haunted every day by the same regret for two decades.

I consistently prayed for Michael for two and a half years before we ever had a conversation about anything spiritual. I believe my prayers allowed God's Spirit to work inside me to grow my compassion for Michael and create the opportunity for him to finally want to talk. God's Spirit was at work in my friend to help him recognize he was stuck in his regret. Here's some of what led up to that conversation—and how God used the B.L.E.S.S. strategy to help my friend come to know the love of God and follow Jesus.

During one cross-country meet, Michael said to me, "Hey, I'd like for us to talk sometime. I've got some stuff I'm trying to work out." I quickly agreed, and we set a date for the first of several breakfast appointments.

As I sat across from him at one of our favorite diners, he looked at me with tears in his eyes and began to share with me a story he had only told his wife up to that point. With obvious emotion, he began to unburden his soul from the pain and shame he had carried for years.

"When I was in grad school out in California, my best friend was a guy named Jay. He was a really good guy. The kind of guy I always aspired to be. I was the best man in his wedding, and since I was newly engaged, I wanted him to be the best man in my wedding."

Michael paused to compose himself. He took a sip of coffee and a bite of toast and continued. "Dave, it was exactly twenty years ago today that we were in a car accident. I survived. Jay did not. I watched him die in that car crash. It was all my fault. His parents refused to speak to me and held me responsible for his death. They wanted nothing to do with me. Every day since, I have lived with the guilt and shame of that moment. I decided to never tell anyone. So for twenty years, I have felt like I had the burden of not just living one life, but two—my own and Jay's—in a futile effort to somehow make up for his loss."

After our conversation, I felt like the forgiveness Michael needed would come when he discovered he was not alone in dealing with his regrets. So I invited him to my small group as we were going through a book Jon and I had written called *Starting Over* (Multnomah, 2016). It was the perfect big idea for Michael. He agreed to come and bring his wife, Stacie. I knew it would be a good experience for him, but I underestimated just how good.

At the last minute, several people had scheduling conflicts and were not able to make it to our group that night, so it ended up being just six of us gathered in our living room: my wife, Sue, and I, Michael and his wife, and our friends the Kings. The Kings had their own story of tragically losing their daughter, Chelsea, who was murdered at the age of seventeen. It was an unusually small group that night, and while pastors rarely like to see a decline in attendance of any kind, God knew exactly what He was doing with only the six of us there.

About fifteen minutes into our discussion, the Kings began to share their story of having to start over after losing Chelsea. As they spoke about forgiveness and redemption in the middle of the most regrettable situation, you could feel God transforming our living room into a holy place. The Spirit of God was clearly present.

The Kings finished their story, and then Michael spoke.

"First, I'm so sorry," he said to the Kings. "I didn't know..." Then he continued, "The two of you are so brave..." Hearing someone with a story that was at least as painful as his own gave him the courage to share it. He began to talk about that day twenty years ago, the accident, Jay's death, and the burden of trying to live two lives. For the second time in two weeks, he was sharing his story out loud with someone other than his wife, and he was discovering the release and refreshment of forgiveness.

A couple days later, Michael called me and explained that he had shared his story of finding forgiveness with several people we both knew. He said, "Dave, every time I share my story, it's like my burden gets lighter and lighter!" Then he said, "Hey Dave, I want to be baptized, and since my birthday is on Easter this year, I want my son Austin and you to baptize me!"

On Easter morning, Michael shared his story with our whole church family.

"I did not have a relationship with God," he said. "I did not think about it. Having a relationship with God was not a goal or objective of mine. My mentality was if you want to get something done, you could only rely on you! And that is how I approached the world for many years."

He went on to give the details of the accident and his decisions since that time. "It didn't matter how hard I tried or what I accomplished—something was still missing. I just kept walking through life carrying what felt like a bag of bricks. I never considered that I could put them down or ask for help.

"Then I got invited to go to a small group. I didn't really know what that was because I'd never been in a small group. I was very nervous. And I was nervous because the group was about regret. I remember thinking, *How appropriate that my first small group is about the very subject I need to learn the most about.*

"For most of my life, I thought that asking for help was a sign of weakness. What I have come to realize is that asking for help is a sign of strength. If you really want some help, the best place you can go is to ask God for help and accept Jesus into your life."

Then—surrounded by family, friends he had invited from across the country, and his new small group—Michael was baptized. As a pastor, I had baptized lots of people, but Michael was my *friend*. I cannot tell you how good it felt to get to help one of my friends come to know God's love and follow Jesus. What a blessing it was to be a blessing to him!

That is exactly what I want for you. Madeleine L'Engle explained how this can occur: "We draw people to Christ not by loudly discrediting what they believe, by telling them how wrong they are and how right we are, but by showing them a light that is so lovely that they want with all their hearts to know the source of it."[1]

So let's move on to the next chapter to check out how this world-changing starts with the first B.L.E.S.S. practice that you cannot skip if you want to see your friends' lives and eternities transformed.

B.L.E.S.S. Discussion Questions

OPEN: What images or thoughts come to mind when you hear the words "evangelize" and "convert"?

_____

_____

_____

_____

DIG: Are you more naturally a "blesser" or "converter" when it comes to reaching people who are far from God?

_____

_____

_____

_____

_____

_____

Read Genesis 12:1-3, Luke 19:1-10, and Galatians 3:7-9. What do these passages tell you about God's plan for His people to be a blessing to those around us?

_____

_____

_____

_____

_____

Based on the brief descriptions in this chapter, which of these five B.L.E.S.S. practices do you think will come easiest to you? Which will require more effort for you to put into action?

_____

_____

_____

_____

How could simply being a B.L.E.S.S.Ing be a strategy for loving our neighbors and changing the world?

_____

_____

_____

_____

What do you find most interesting or encouraging about Michael's story of finding his way back to God?

_____

_____

_____

_____

_____

REFLECT: Who in your life has been the greatest B.L.E.S.S.ing to you in your spiritual journey? How can you begin to emulate his or her approach as you seek to reach the people around you?

_____

_____

_____

_____

_____

_____

_____

_____

_____

_____

_____

_____

CHAPTER 3

B: Begin with Prayer

BIG IDEA
To B.L.E.S.S. your neighbor, Jesus invites you
to begin with prayer.

I cannot change the world.

You cannot change the world.

Even prayer alone doesn't change the world.

Only God can change the world!

However, God uses prayer to change us, and then God uses us to change our world.

Let God Talk

My meeting had finished early, and I left the group and headed to a soft chair on the other side of the room. It was January, and I was in South Florida for a board meeting (a great place to be that time of year if you live in Chicago!). I reached into my computer bag and pulled out my journal and Bible. After spending some time reading and reflecting, my routine was to first write the word "B.L.E.S.S." and then list the people for whom I would simply pray for a few minutes.

Prayer is like breathing.

Breathing has the rhythm of inhaling and then exhaling. We breathe in the oxygen we need and then exhale carbon dioxide that the plants around us need. It's this rhythm of inhaling and exhaling that brings life both to us and to our planet. Without oxygen, we would die. Without carbon dioxide, our green world would shrivel up and also die.

Prayer is the same. We breathe in to listen to God; we need His voice to sustain our spiritual life (John 8:47). We then breathe out a missional prayer for our neighbors, anticipating that it will bring spiritual life to them.

Next, I drew a straight black line across the bottom of the page in my journal, paused, and then listened for God. This is how I've learned to pray every day. Drawing that horizontal line became a ritual that transitioned my mind from *talking* to God to *listening* to Him. Often when I listen, nothing comes to mind—but if something or someone does, I write it down.

That day this came to mind: "Ask Ron how he's doing." The question just popped into my head.

I hadn't thought about Ron in weeks, but I knew he would be joining me for another meeting later in the day. I wrote "Ask Ron how he's doing" in my journal.

About five minutes later, Ron walked into the room. He had decided to stop in early. I felt myself smiling. *That was fast!* I got up from my easy chair and crossed the room to greet him.

Ron asked, "Got some time to hang out?"

We spent the next hour catching up. When there was a pause in the conversation, I asked him, "How are you doing?" The pause became a silence. He looked away and said, "Not so good…" He went on to explain how he had just lost his job. It was not a good transition, and he hadn't confided in anyone other than his wife about how he really felt.

Later I was able to explain to Ron that I felt like God had brought him to my mind while praying. The conversation, some compassion, and the very idea that God brought his name to my mind were all very meaningful to Ron.

Simple, everyday ways to love your neighbor. God wants to do that kind of stuff...a lot!

Love Begins with Prayer

Marco had heard me teach on the B.L.E.S.S. practices and began to pray for his friend Victoria. Victoria was far from God, but she was searching. At a very young age her family quit attending church, and by the time she was an adolescent, she had experienced so much pain that even if there was a God, she reasoned, He wasn't a nice guy. So during middle school, she began to tell people she was an atheist, and her Christian friends felt obliged to inform her, "Victoria, you are going to Hell!"

Her young adulthood was filled with searching for what was missing. She got married, but then cheated on her husband and destroyed the relationship. She decided to move far from home where she sought out happiness in sexual adventures that ultimately ruined her emotionally, relationally, and financially.

Victoria met Marco after moving back to where she grew up. He began to pray for her and listen to her story of searching. Their friendship was slowly turning into a romance.

Marco had the wisdom not to push faith, Jesus, or God on Victoria. He understood that he was to be the salt of the earth, but also that rubbing salt into a wound like she had would be very painful. So he helped Victoria heal.

Victoria began to ask Marco questions about spiritual things, and Marco asked her if she would like to go to church. She was very skittish about being around Christians; the voices of her middle school friends still echoed. He reassured her it wouldn't be like that, and eventually, she showed up at church—unsure, but with an open heart.

Over the next few weeks, Victoria not only went to church but also joined a small group that ate together every week. This group became friends, and in time it became a transforming community in her life. She later said, "What I found in that group were some genuinely amazing people. It was those people who helped me find my way back to God."

There are a couple reasons I will never forget the day that Marco baptized Victoria. First, because she courageously told the whole church her heart-breaking but beautiful story—and after she was baptized, the people she feared would judge her gave her a raucous standing ovation. And second, because I got to see Marco use simple, everyday ways of B.L.E.S.S.ing to love his friend to salvation.

That blessing turned into a mutual one when Victoria and Marco got married. And Marco's simple prayer for Victoria grew into a beautiful family with three children.

Crazy Things Begin with Prayer

It was Holocaust survivor Corrie ten Boom who said, "We never know how God will answer our prayers, but we can expect that He will get us involved in His plan for the answer." I believe that! Sometimes when God gets us involved, outlandish and powerful stuff begins to happen. A couple of my favorite stories come from Louie and Dean.

One day Louie went to the mall, and for whatever reason he noticed a guy sitting on a bench. He said he had a strange sensation: *Go tell that guy God loves him.* Of course, Louie didn't want to do that. (Would you want to walk up to someone you don't know at all and say, "Hey, God loves you"?) So he did what most of us might: he shrugged it off and kept on shopping.

When Louie came out of a store in another part of the mall a bit later, there was that same guy again. Again, Louie felt an inner nudge. *Go over there and tell him God loves him.* He blew it off again.

Then a third time, he saw the same guy. Again, he got the same prompting. Finally, he said, "Alright!" He walked up to the guy and said, "I don't want to seem weird or anything, but I feel like I'm supposed to tell you that God loves you."

Immediately, the stranger's eyes filled up with tears, and he said, "This morning I was at the end of my rope. I told God, 'If You're real, show me You love me today.' I don't know who you are, but you're the third random person in the mall today who's come up to me and said 'Hey, I don't know you, but God loves you.' No one's ever said it to me once before, and now it's happened three times in one day."

I have a hunch that God is speaking to us in similar ways all the time, but we're only listening some of the time. What if instead of waiting for God to grab our attention, we were intentional about giving it to Him? What if we began each day with a prayer to be a blessing to our neighbors and asked God for divine appointments?

My friend Dean, who works in college ministry at a large state university, has made it a practice over the years to begin every day that way. His prayer is very simply that he would meet and talk to people God wants him to bless. And then he just goes through his day assuming that whomever he talks to might be that divine appointment.

I remember one story he told me about someone canceling an appointment with him. Instead of filling the time with emails or an Instagram post, he decided to pray. He asked, "God, how do You want me to use this time?" As he sat still, listening to God, the name of a student, "Janice," came to him. He sensed he was supposed to talk to her about Jesus. Janice had never been to church and was not a Christ-follower, but she had been to a college small group a couple times. So he called and asked to connect over coffee. She said, "Sure."

When they met, he just told her, "Janice, I was praying and your name came to mind, and I felt like I was supposed to share with you how you can become a follower of Jesus."

Janice stood there in silence. First came a tear…and then sobbing.

Dean immediately recoiled and said, "Oh, I'm sorry. I shouldn't have just blurted that out…did I say something that offended you?"

"No. Not at all," Janice said. "I just can't believe you said that. Last night I decided to go to a Bible study in my dorm. They were talking about what it means to be a Christian, and I couldn't stop thinking about it. All night, I couldn't sleep. I didn't know what to do about it. So I prayed this morning, asking God to bring someone to me today to tell me how to become a Christian." She smiled and said, "And here you are. I just can't believe it!"

I love talking to Dean because every single day of his life is an adventure. I'm not kidding! Every day, this guy seeks to find how God can use him to bless the world, and he begins with prayer. I want you to take note of this: for Dean, prayer is both how you discover the mission and how you pursue it!

Jesus Begins with Prayer

You know why Dean does this? Because Jesus did it! Prayer was not only how Jesus began His day; it was how He began His whole ministry. In his account of Jesus's life, Luke wrote in Chapter 4, *"Then Jesus, being filled with the Holy Spirit, returned from the Jordan and was led by the Spirit into the wilderness."* Jesus went off into the wilderness to fast and pray and confront the evil one. Prayer was how He began His mission on Earth.

Two chapters later, when Jesus was getting ready to select those who would join Him on this mission, look what Luke 6 says He did:

"One of those days Jesus went out to a mountainside to pray, and spent the night praying to God. When morning came, he called his disciples to him and chose twelve of them, whom he also designated

apostles: Simon (whom he named Peter), his brother Andrew, James, John, Philip, Bartholomew, Matthew, Thomas, James son of Alphaeus, Simon who was called the Zealot, Judas son of James, and Judas Iscariot, who betrayed Him." (Luke 6:12–16 NIV)

If that had been me, I might have been tempted to skip the prayer part and just pick the guys I liked the most or who seemed to be the most gifted. You think there weren't a few obvious first-round draft picks? Of course there were! But Jesus didn't just do what made sense to Him; He spent the night in prayer before deciding on the twelve He would invest His life in and disciple. The stakes were high. These twelve would be the first ones He would bless with His life, and together they would form a community of friendship. Once they were ready, Jesus would send them out to bless the world.

You see, it's always been God's dream to bless the world through His people, and originally, His people were the twelve tribes of ancient Israel. But along the way, they kept focusing on themselves, their needs, and their status as God's chosen people. They didn't understand that the mission wasn't just for them to be blessed, but to be a blessing!

But God didn't give up on His dream of a people who would love one another and share His love. As Jesus blessed the twelve, He was renewing God's mission to the world. Scholars will tell you that these twelve people are kind of "replacements" for the twelve tribes. God was starting over, renewing His plan for the twelve tribes through these twelve soon-to-be apostles who would take the blessing to others.

Now, some of you might be ahead of me, wondering, *Why does Jesus need to pray if He's God?* Good question! Two reasons…

First, even though Jesus was God in the flesh, to become a human being meant taking on self-imposed limitations. The Bible says He knows what it is like to be us, to be in our shoes, and so He became a lot more like us than most of us have ever imagined. Even as God in the flesh, He depended on God the Father and looked to Him for direction.

Second, Jesus lived a life that would be an example for us of how to be fully human and how we should live. In the same way that He taught

Prayer also changes you.

If you are not regularly praying for people by name, I doubt God will use you to help change them. I believe this for two reasons: First, God has chosen to work through us so that "they may see your good works and give glory to your Father who is in heaven" (Matthew 5:14–16). So prayer is connecting to the Source that will bring change in others. Second, prayer is connecting to the Source that will change you! When you begin with prayer, God begins to change your heart, and you begin to feel what God feels for other people. They are no longer projects. When God's Spirit allows you to feel what God feels, you get ideas that come from God, like "Send a text to your neighbor to see how he's doing" or "Ask your friend if she's got time for coffee this week." When they ask you, "What's up?" you just say, "I was praying and just thought of you." Often, the timing of those promptings to reach out is remarkable. Many times, I've heard people tell me, "Wow, your timing is crazy!" It's because God uses prayer to change others, but He also uses it to change you!

the disciples to pray through the Lord's Prayer, He taught us to live by how He lived His life on Earth.

We don't know exactly what happened as Jesus was praying about the twelve disciples. Did the Father speak to Him in an audible voice and start naming names? Did certain names just pop into His head? Was there some sort of sign? The Bible does not tell us.

We only know that before Jesus began His mission to bless the world, He began with prayer. Prayer that He would do what God wanted Him to do. Prayer that God would lead Him to the right people to catalyze a movement of love.

It's interesting to note that the guys Jesus picked after praying weren't the obvious choices for a starting lineup. Instead, they were...

...common fishermen.

...corrupt tax collectors.

...some violent political revolutionaries.

...and a lot of them were just nobodies.

People we would have probably ignored or not noticed.

But Jesus began with prayer.

"Don't Make Me..."

Remember what I said about how God uses prayer to change us and then uses us to change our world? Sometimes God uses us even when we don't want to do what He's asking. Bible teacher Beth Moore tells a story that I will never forget about how prayer forced her to do something she really didn't want to do.

As she tells it, she was in the middle of hustling to make her next flight when she stopped for a moment and opened her Bible. After reading a chapter, she paused to pray. Glancing up, Beth noticed an old man sitting in a wheelchair. He was abnormally thin and slumped over, but the strangest thing about him was his hair. Stringy, tangled hair hung well past his shoulders and down his back.

She tried to stop staring, but something in her began to stir with emotion for this bizarre-looking old man. In her words:

> I had walked with God long enough to see the handwriting on the wall. I've learned that when I begin to feel what God feels, something so contrary to my natural feelings, something dramatic is bound to happen. I immediately began to resist. I started arguing with God in my mind. *Oh no, God please no.... Don't make me witness to this man.*

Then I heard it…*I don't want you to witness to him. I want you to brush his hair.*

The words were so clear, my heart leapt into my throat, and my thoughts spun like a top.

After several agonizing moments trying to reason with God that this prompting was ridiculous, a red-faced and tentative Beth approached the old man and knelt down before him.

"May I have the pleasure of brushing your hair?" she asked.

To which he responded in volume set at ten, "Little lady, if you expect me to hear you, you're going to have to talk louder than that."

At this point, I took a deep breath and blurted out, "SIR, MAY I HAVE THE PLEASURE OF BRUSHING YOUR HAIR?" At which point every eye in the place darted right at me.

I watched him look up at me with absolute shock on his face, and say, "If you really want to." Are you kidding? Of course I didn't want to. But God didn't seem interested in my personal preference right about then. "Yes, sir, I would be pleased. But I have one little problem. I don't have a hairbrush."

"I have one in my bag," he responded.

Beth went to the back of the stranger's wheelchair, unzipped the old carry-on to retrieve the hairbrush, and started brushing the old man's hair. She continues…

A miraculous thing happened to me as I started brushing that old man's hair.… Everybody else seemed to disappear. There was no one alive for those moments except that old man and me. I brushed and brushed and I brushed until every tangle was out. I know this sounds so strange, but I've never felt that kind of love for another soul in my entire life. I believe with all my heart, I—for that few minutes—felt a portion of the very love of God.... The emotions were so strong and so pure that I knew they had to be God's.

His hair was finally as soft and smooth as an infant's. I slipped the brush back in the bag, went around the chair to face him. I got back down on my knees, put my hands on his knees, and said, "Sir, do you know my Jesus?"

He said, "Yes, I do. I've known Him since I married my bride. She wouldn't marry me until I got to know the Savior." He said, "You see, the problem is, I haven't seen my bride in months. I've had open-heart surgery, and she's been too ill to come see me. I was sitting here thinking to myself what a mess I must be for my bride."

Beth concludes:

Only God knows how often He allows us to be part of a divine moment when we're completely unaware of the significance. God had intervened in details only He could have known. It was a God moment, and I'll never forget it.[1]

Ready for an Adventure?

How do you feel when you hear stories like Beth's? Or Dean's? Or Louie's? Sure, many of us are touched. We might even tear up a little. But is anyone else besides me willing to admit that stories like this are also a little terrifying? Sure, we love to hear them when they're about *other* people, but we're not so sure we want to find *ourselves* doing crazy things like this.

I'm going to be straight-up with you: If you and I are going to be blessings to the people around us and take the mission of Jesus seriously, we are in for an adventure.

There's no telling where God might send us or what He might lead us to do. Following Jesus isn't meant to be comfortable; it's meant to be life-changing!

Reasons We Don't Pray

Your adventure with God begins with prayer. But prayer is one of those things—like flossing or exercise or going to bed at a decent hour—that we know we should do but often don't do.

Every time I go to the dentist, he asks me if I'm flossing regularly. I don't want to tell him I'm not doing what I know I should do, so I say something like, "I'm flossing the same amount as the last time you asked me." (It's not a lie!)

Prayer can be like that for most of us. It's something we know we should do, something we even *want* to do, but it can be hard to be consistent with it. Why is that? I can think of a lot of reasons.

"I don't know how to pray."

Sometimes we don't pray because we don't know how. Many of us learned to pray as children—mostly at meals and at bedtime. You know, "Now I lay me down to sleep ..." Or "Yubba dub dub, thanks for the grub. Yay, God!" But how many people reach adulthood without any additional instruction? We know we should pray, but many of us aren't sure how.

"I'm too busy."

Sometimes we don't pray because life is too busy. Let's face it...prayer takes time, it takes focus, it takes energy, and many of us feel like we're running short on all those things. Our busy lives crowd out a lot of things we know are important, and often that includes prayer.

"I doubt it works."

And sometimes we don't pray because we are not sure it works. Maybe you are thinking, *I prayed, I really did, and it didn't seem to make any difference.* I've felt that way before. When we pray and nothing seems to happen, it makes it really difficult to keep on praying.

There are lots of reasons why we don't pray, but I'm challenging you: if you want to change your neighborhood and change your world, you have to begin with prayer. Let me make this as clear as I can because what we are talking about is a very big deal! Your neighbors' and friends' lives and eternities are at stake! My experience is that when there is something really big and important at stake—like a tragedy—at that moment we all know how to pray! We definitely aren't too busy to pray during a crisis. And our attitude in the moment is "Let's see if it works." So if nothing else, I encourage you to start there!

How to Begin with Prayer

Jesus is the One we follow. His whole life was a blessing to the world. Every place He went, every person He encountered experienced a "God moment" in His presence. Jesus lived out the B.L.E.S.S. practices in His daily life on Earth, and He did that by beginning with prayer.

I know it's risky and can feel uncomfortable, but only God knows the impact you and I can make in someone's life when we choose to be a B.L.E.S.S.ing. And it all begins with prayer.

In prayer, we open ourselves to God and the leading of His Spirit.

In prayer, we focus our minds to recognize His promptings.

In prayer, we receive the direction we need to discover the people God is calling us to bless.

"Who Is My Neighbor?" Map

This first tool is a simple way to get you started right now in praying for your neighbors. It's called the "Who Is My Neighbor?" map. It was given to us by Jay Pathak and Dave Runyon in their book *The Art of Neighboring*—a great companion to the book you are reading.

Photocopy the "Who Is My Neighbor?" graphic or simply sketch one out on the back of a napkin or in your journal if you use one. The center square represents where you live. The eight surrounding houses represent your neighbors. Write each of your neighbors' names in the surrounding eight squares. Don't get hung up on being geographically accurate; just think about the eight people who live closest to you. This works if you live in an urban apartment or townhouse, a suburban cul-de-sac, or out in the country. Just ask "Who is my neighbor?" and write in their names.

If you do not know the names of your eight closest neighbors, then find out. Google them. Ask them. Whatever you have to do, you must know their names and write them in the boxes. Then use this tool to begin praying for eight people in close geographical proximity to you.

This tool can also be used to identify your neighbors in other settings too. If you want to use it for work, just ask "Who are the eight people in closest physical or relational proximity to me at work?" You can do the same with where you play. For example, ask "Who are eight other people on my team?" or "Who are eight other people I regularly see at the gym?" Once you know their names, begin with prayer.

So now my challenge to you is to set aside some time every day to pray for each of these eight people by name. I'm not asking you to pray all night like Jesus did, but we can all start somewhere.

In time you will find that you won't need the "Who Is Your Neighbor?" map because you have memorized the names of these eight people that God is asking you to love. But this simple tool is a great way to get you started in praying for the neighbors where you live, work, or play.

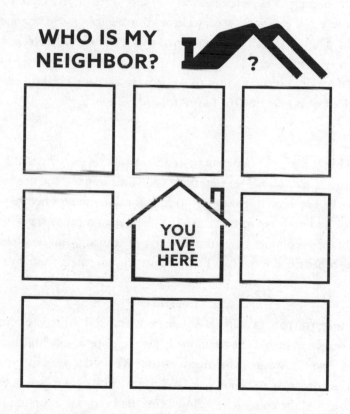

Hudson Taylor, a British missionary to China, said, "Do not have your concert first, and then tune your instrument afterwards. Begin the day with the Word of God and prayer, and get first of all into harmony with Him."[2]

I love that! For us to love our neighbor we have to be in harmony with Him. That begins with prayer.

Five Simple B.L.E.S.S. Tools

In chapters three through seven I will give you a simple tool that goes along with each of the five B.L.E.S.S. practices. Each of these corresponding tools is designed so you can immediately put into practice these five everyday ways to love your neighbor and change your world. These tools are meant to turn this from a good book you read to a way of life every day!

To make sure you use this tool everyday and don't just fill out it out and forget about it, use the four P's listed below:

Plan

Things that are important to us are written on our calendars. If you want to be intentional about setting aside time to pray, you need to plan for it. Perhaps you might decide to pray for five minutes before you get out of bed and five minutes at night before you go to sleep. Or you might set a reminder on your phone to pray during your lunch hour or some other time of the day. Plan to pray for your neighbors by name.

Prepare

Next, you need to prepare. As you pray, ask God to prepare your heart for the adventure. As I've mentioned, if we're going to take the mission of Jesus seriously, we are in for an adventure! We need to prepare our hearts for the adventure to come. Ask God to give you eyes to see how He is leading and the courage to follow Him. Be bold: ask Him to give you divine appointments with each of the people named, as well as others.

Places

As you pray, make a mental map of the places you'll visit during the day. Ask God to help you be sensitive to your surroundings and guide you to places where He wants you to be a blessing.

People

Finally, ask God to show you how to be a blessing to your eight neighbors. As you pray, envision the faces of each of your neighbors and ask God to show you how you can be a blessing in their lives today.

Remember that when you pray for people you are already blessing them. A while back a friend of mine challenged me in this way. He asked me, "Do you realize that there are people you come across every day who have never once had someone pray for them?" His question took me by surprise. I grew up in a Christ-following home. My parents have been praying for me from the moment the pregnancy test revealed I had been conceived. What a blessing that has been to me.

You can offer that same blessing to your friends and neighbors when you pray for them. Pray for their physical health, their relationships, their emotional well-being, their careers, and their finances. Just think of how you would want someone to pray for you and start praying for them in the very same ways.

It's Life-Changing!

Following Jesus isn't meant to be comfortable; it's meant to be life-changing! There's no telling where He might send us and what He might lead us to do!

Sure, we are moved by stories about hairbrushes and divine appointments, but imagine what it will be like to not just *hear* those stories, but to actually *live* them.

And to do that, let's begin with prayer.

The next B.L.E.S.S. practice is one of the most practical—and powerful—ways you can love someone. It's something Jesus did well and often. In fact, he did it so well and so often because He wanted to show us how simple it was—and how it could change someone's life forever. Intrigued? Turn the page.

B.L.E.S.S. Discussion Questions

OPEN: What are your earliest memories of praying? Did you recite a particular prayer? Did you pray in a specific place or with particular people?

_____

_____

_____

_____

_____

DIG: Right after Jesus was baptized but before He began His ministry, He went into the wilderness to fast and pray (Luke 4). In Luke 6:12–16, we find that He prayed before He selected His disciples. What do you notice from these examples about the emphasis Jesus placed on time alone with God in prayer?

_____

_____

_____

_____

What do you find most challenging about prayer?

_____

_____

_____

_____

When have you found prayer to be most helpful?

_____

_____

_____

Prayer is a conversation in which we talk to God and He talks to us. Have you ever felt a prompting from God to reach out to someone? How did you respond? What was the result?

_____

_____

_____

REFLECT: Who are the people you can begin to pray for, asking God to give you opportunities to B.L.E.S.S. them?

_____

_____

_____

Use the B.L.E.S.S. tool provided to write down the names of eight neighbors where you live, work, or play. Then begin with prayer!

_____

_____

_____

_____

_____

CHAPTER 4

L: Listen

BIG IDEA
To B.L.E.S.S. your neighbor, Jesus invites you to listen.

I bet you know someone (or maybe you are someone) who has a special knack for singing the wrong lyrics to a song. I remember when I realized that "el-em-en-oh" wasn't a word, but was actually the four letters that precede "P" in the alphabet song.

I also remember when I heard someone sing Bon Jovi's "Livin' on a Prayer" at the top of their lungs, shouting, "It doesn't make a difference if we're naked or not." (That someone will remain nameless.) Fun fact: this phenomenon actually has a name—a mondegreen. It's a misheard word or phrase that makes sense in your head, but which is entirely incorrect.

Of course, one of the classic songs for mondegreens is Manfred Mann's Earth Band's "Blinded by the Light." Is there anyone who didn't sing "a little hurly burly made my anus curly whirly and she asked me if I needed a ride"? Can't explain it!

I'm sure you can think of your own mondegreen moments. They give us some great examples of how important listening is.

There are four H's of listening.

The best salespeople in the world are not smooth talkers, but rather are great listeners. Listening is not a talent some are born with and some are not. It is a skill that we develop and get better at over time. So how do you develop it? One way is to come prepared to every conversation to use the four H's of listening. These are categories of questions that you can always ask:

History: "Tell me your story." "Where did you grow up?

Heart: "What's your favorite (team, restaurant, vacation destination)?"

Habits: "What are you into?" "What do you like to do with your free time?"

Hurts: "How are you doing with (name the situation)?"

These types of questions will help you become a great listener. And that allows you to become a better friend to your neighbors.

In the last chapter, I challenged you to begin with prayer—the first step in B.L.E.S.S.ing others. In this chapter, I'm going to focus on the second practice: Listen. As I said earlier, any relationship starts with listening to someone's words and life. And really hearing and understanding what someone you've been praying for is saying and feeling may be the kindest and most loving gift you can give to someone. David W. Augsburger said in *Caring Enough to Hear and Be Heard*: "Being heard is as close to being loved that for the average person, they are almost indistinguishable."[1] Listening moves us forward in our relationships as God uses us to bless others and change their lives. It's the next step in loving your neighbors and helping them know the love of God.

Not Really Listening

You and I live in a world where hardly anybody really listens to each other. You don't have to look much further than social media to see that most people are more interested in what *they* have to say than what someone else has to say. I often think about this saying: "The opposite of listening is not speaking. It's waiting to speak."

Isn't that true? That even when we're not talking, we can simply be waiting for our turn to talk—and not actually listening to the words someone else is saying? I don't like admitting this, but too many times, I'll be in the middle of a conversation, and I'm not really listening. I'm just cuing up what I'm going to say next. If you think about it, I bet you do it too.

We probably all also understand what it's like to be on the other end—the one who's not listened to, who feels unheard. How many times have you been in a conversation with a person who was there but not *really* there? Lots of "uh-huhs" on the other end.

I want you to try something. Try to be silent for twenty seconds and pay attention to what you hear. OK? Twenty seconds of silence where you listen for even the faintest noise. Ready?...Go!

Now make a list of what you heard.

Did you hear a car drive by, a bird chirping, your house creaking? The furnace or air conditioner kicking on?

Here's the truth: You were hearing all of that before. For as long as you've been sitting reading this book, you've been hearing all sorts of noises, but a lot of them went unheard because you weren't really listening! That happens with the people in our lives too. A lot of what they are saying goes unheard because we aren't really listening.

And when we don't listen, people not only feel unheard, but begin to feel unknown.

The other day, I had to call an airline for customer support. (I know, who calls customer support these days thinking they'll actually get the help they need?) But I was desperate. Only fifteen seconds after I dialed the 1-800 number, I got the dreaded automated message: "If you need help with blah, blah, blah, press one; for all other questions, press two."

None of those options were what I needed. Just when I was about to hang up, I got the computer voice: "Your call is important to us…please stay on the line …" I wanted to scream, "It's *not* important to you; otherwise a real person would get on the line!"

And yet, we all do this. When a friend, coworker, or maybe a neighbor comes to you needing to talk about something, rather than listening to understand, we jump into "fix-it" mode by giving them two or three options for making it right. The truth is that most people don't want your expertise; they want your support. They just want to be heard, known, and to know you care.

Here is the real issue: When the people in our lives feel unheard and unknown, it ultimately leaves them feeling unloved.

unheard + **unknown** = **unloved**

If you want to love your neighbors and bless the people God has put in your path, you have to become intentional about listening and listening to understand.

Jesus as a Listener

Jesus was the ultimate listener. He modeled this second B.L.E.S.S. practice for us in amazing ways. He was motivated by love for every person He encountered. Not only did He perform great miracles and teach mind-blowing truths, but Jesus also took the time, again and again, to show love in the most practical and simple way: He listened.

Learn to be a great listener.

Some of the B.L.E.S.S practices will come more naturally than others. One of the most difficult skills to develop is listening. There are at least four types of noise that make it hard for us to listen to others: 1) physical noise that happens in the setting, 2) psychological noise that happens in our minds, 3) physiological noise that happens because we are feeling something in our bodies, and 4) semantic noise because we get confused by the meaning of the speaker's words. To really become a great listener requires us to block out those distractions. And when there are semantic misunderstandings, we ask the person to clarify them for us. You can become a great listener, but it requires a lot more intention than most of us think.

Luke's account of Jesus and the blind beggar is a great example:

When Jesus was coming close to Jericho, a blind man sat begging beside the road. The man heard the crowd walking by and asked what was happening. Some people told him that Jesus from Nazareth was passing by. So the blind man shouted, "Jesus, Son of David, have pity on me!" The people who were going along with Jesus told the man to be quiet. But he shouted even louder, "Son of David, have pity on me!" Jesus stopped and told some people to bring the blind man over to him. (Luke 18:35–40 NLT)

Pause a minute with me because I don't want you to miss this. Jesus wasn't necessarily looking for someone to heal that day. He was on his way to Jericho, one of the last stops on the way to Jerusalem to participate in the Passover Feast.

Jericho was extra-busy that time of year. Picture Times Square on New Year's Eve. Hordes of people. And in the midst of them was a blind man crying out in all the noise, "Have mercy on me!"

In all that commotion, Jesus heard that singular voice. It makes me think of how my wife, Sue, could hear even the faintest cry of one of our kids at night when I was lying next to her, oblivious.

Jesus heard the blind man the same way. The people traveling with Him told the man to leave Jesus alone. But he wouldn't. Instead, he cried out even louder. And here's what happened next:

> Jesus asked (the man), "What do you want me to do for you?" "Lord, I want to see!' he answered. Jesus replied, "Look and you will see! Your eyes are healed because of your faith." (Luke 18:40–42 CEV)

You knew that was coming, right? Blind man can't see, He calls out to Jesus, and Jesus heals him. The end.

But not so fast: What I want you to notice is the question Jesus asks: "What do you want me to do for you?" Seems like a silly question, doesn't it? I'm sure Jesus knew the man was blind, so why does He ask him that? Is this some sort of dramatic buildup for the miracle to follow? I don't think so. I believe something is happening here that we could easily miss in a quick read.

This question Jesus asks tells us something profound about His character. It shows that Jesus didn't assume He knew what people needed—and He didn't want you or me to assume we know what people need either. So He asked questions and listened.

You want to bless your neighbors, friends, and family? Imitate Jesus in the way you listen to them. It's a challenge not just to hear the words they say, but to really listen. Put down your smartphone.

Turn off Netflix. Slow down the busyness and give them your full attention.

Because that's how you really get to know the people in your life.

Ultimately, when you take the time to listen and get to know someone, that's when the people around you truly feel loved and blessed.

listen + **being known** = **loved**

When I flip through the accounts of Jesus's life and ministry in Matthew, Mark, Luke, and John, the achiever in me is naturally drawn to the stories of Jesus doing over-the-top, amazing feats like healing the sick, feeding thousands of hungry people, and even raising the dead. I tend to remember the exceptional and extraordinary moments. But as I've looked at Jesus's life and how He modeled these B.L.E.S.S. practices, His more frequent and ordinary interactions started to jump out at me. The moments when He paused, pulled up a chair, looked someone in the eye, and simply *listened*.

I don't want you to miss this: Living a life of blessing others like Jesus did is not a journey of the spectacular. In fact, it's usually best lived out in the regular. In the everyday. In these seemingly mundane moments of life, we can get within arm's reach of another person and actually listen to what's going on in their hearts and thoughts. That's when we may have our greatest opportunity to love and bless someone.

Listening across Cultures

My friend Michael Frost illustrates the power of listening in a story he tells about a missionary group who went to India to serve the poor in a remote village. The group showed up with all sorts of supplies,

Don't buy the cheap stuff

(My friend Rick Richardson shared this story so well that I figured we'd let him tell it in his own words.)

My wife, Mary Kay, and I live in a high-rise condo building in the city; half of the couples on our floor are gay. Since I try to live out these B.L.E.S.S. practices with the people around me, I began praying for the people on my floor. For me, that includes listening for God's promptings and nudges. So as I prayed for my neighbors, I sensed the Holy Spirit nudging me to buy a bottle of wine for one couple down the hall and invite them over for appetizers. So I did just that. And let me say that I bought them a *very* good bottle of wine. I have found that if you don't buy the cheap stuff, it really builds trust.

We had a great time that evening talking and sharing life with each other. It wasn't too long until they invited us over to their place for a meal. During that evening together, Mary Kay and I shared some of our marriage struggles, how we were working through them together, and some of our theories about what makes a relationship truly work. And not so surprisingly, as we shared, our new friends also shared about some struggles they were experiencing.

Not long after that, one of them approached us and asked if he could get some help with his relationship. I'll confess, I felt like I was in over my head. But I continued to pray and ask God for direction. As we listened to our friend's struggles, we decided to meet with him and see if we could offer some additional help. We prayed for him, shared from our experiences, and gave him a book that he read on a personal retreat. It was truly amazing to see God begin to work in his life through these B.L.E.S.S. practices. And as we got to know the couple more, they began to bless us and help us out by watching our condo while we were out of town. When our friend returned from his retreat, we actually started discussing the parable of the Prodigal Son together.

Keep in mind, this didn't happen overnight. It was at least eighteen months from the time we first began to get to know each other until we started discussing the Prodigal Son. However, just a couple weeks ago he told us that he wanted Jesus in his life! So he prayed, and in his own words he said he wanted to come back to the Father. He grew up Catholic, so the notion of finding his way *back* to God the Father made a lot of sense to him. He is taking steps to know Christ, and we started a Bible study together.

As I have been trying to really B.L.E.S.S. others for several years now, I have seen my dad come back to Christ, my friend next door come back to Christ, and others who are on a journey of finding their way back to God. It's been an amazing combination of long-term prayers and seeing God do some incredible work in the lives of people I love.

programs, and skilled workers ready to transform that village into a place of health and vitality. They first went to people living in a slum and said, "We could build a medical clinic to help take care of the hurting and sick in your village. We could build a school to provide education so the next generation can work their way out of poverty. We could build a church so you could gather on the weekends and learn about God."

Then they asked, "What do you want us to do for you?"

So far, so good, right? This sounds a lot like the question that Jesus asked the blind beggar. That's when the people of the village responded with something the missionaries were not at all expecting to hear.

"What we really need most is a mailbox," they said.

The missionaries shot back, "A mailbox? We can build you a medical clinic, a school, or a church building, and all you want is your own mailbox?!"

The villagers went on to explain that in India, not having a mailbox means you don't have a ZIP code. And if you don't have a ZIP code, that means you do not exist on a map. Even if you're part of a community of twenty thousand people, if you don't have a ZIP code, you're not recognized—and that means you're ineligible for social services from the government. These villagers wanted an identity, to become a recognized part of their own country.

Had the missionaries not asked the question and listened, they never would have known this was the people's greatest need. It may sound simple, but getting this village a mailbox was no small task. It took the missionaries two years to work through the bureaucracy to get them registered with a ZIP code—but once they did, the village began to transform.

Listening to the Heart

In 1816, René Laennec, a French doctor who was uncomfortable about placing his ear directly on a woman's chest to listen to her heart, invented a tool that doctors continue using today: the stethoscope. He was famous for telling doctors and nurses, "If you use this tool, don't stop listening to your patients—they will still tell you how to heal them." Laennec didn't want doctors to just listen to hearts and lungs with his invention. He wanted to make sure they still listened to the words and feelings of their patients.

I wonder if we understand that we can be a huge gift to others just by listening to their hearts. A writer friend once told me, "Dave, everyone has a story, but few people who will listen to that story." One of the most practical and powerful ways we can be blessings is to simply listen. Listen to people. Listen to our community. Listen to our coworkers. Listen to our classmates. Listen to our neighbors. Listen to the hurts, the needs, and the pain of the people in our lives. Listen to their stories and discover what they really need.

When was the last time you asked the single mom who lives near you how she's doing? Or stopped what you were doing to give your undivided attention to the person in the cubicle next to you? When was the last time you slowed down enough to listen to the cashier who casually mentioned that her husband was hospitalized?

When I say "Listen to people," I don't just mean listen to the words that come out of their mouths. I'm talking about listening to their hearts!

Over twenty years ago, Stephen Covey wrote his landmark self-help book *The 7 Habits of Highly Effective People*. People have bought his book by the millions, including me. And one of the habits I'll never forget is this: "Seek first to understand before seeking to be understood." It reminds me of what God says in this proverb: "It's stupid and embarrassing to give an answer before you listen" (Proverbs 18:3 CEV).

Not My Finest Pastor Moment

You probably have someone in your life who is exhausting to have a conversation with because they just won't stop talking. You have to fight to find even the slightest break in their talking just to get in a word or two.

Several years back, I decided I was going to have a heart-to-heart talk with Joe, the incessant talker in my Sunday group. So one Sunday I said, "Joe, if you would just give people a chance to talk, take a breath between sentences, and not dominate the conversation so much, you might find that people actually want to talk to you more. You just don't let anyone have a chance to say anything!" It seemed like pretty good advice.

As soon as I said it, Joe's demeanor changed. His speech slowed down. He looked down, got very serious, and said, "Dave, the reason I talk so much on Sundays is that this is the only human contact I have in my entire week. The only people I get to converse with Monday through Saturday are the cashiers at the grocery store."

Immediately, I felt a lump rise in my throat. As I listened to his heart, I got to know Joe more. He shared with me that he has no family, no brothers or sisters, no children, no friends to talk to at all. And then he said something I'll never forget: "I'm afraid that if I don't keep talking, act happy and upbeat, then no one will talk to me at all."

Here I was thinking that if I could just let this guy know how he comes across, then Joe would finally understand and change his ways. And while he did have some work to do, the real breakthrough came when I stopped talking and began to listen to his story and his loneliness. Not my most stellar pastor moment.

When it comes to blessing your neighbors, friends, or coworkers, I want to challenge you to listen with intention. You can't assume you know what to do for them. You need to first listen to understand their hurts, their fears, their dreams, their disappointments, their hopes, and their longings. My question to you is: *Are you willing to listen?*

Listening to Places

Not only do I want you to listen to the *people* around you, but I also want you to listen to the heartbeat in the *places* around you. Listening to places requires us to listen in ways that are different from how we listen to people—but no less impactful.

The second half of the book of Acts tells the story of how Paul brought the good news of Jesus to particular cities and towns throughout the lands that are now Turkey and Greece. In Acts 17, Paul found himself in the city of Athens.

The people of Athens consumed new ideas like Chicagoans consume pizza. In the ancient world, Athens was the capital of philosophy. It was a place where the people took pride in their rich cultural heritage.

Luke, the doctor and historian, described the flavor of Athens with a funny statement in Acts 17: "All the Athenians and the foreigners who lived there spent their time doing nothing but talking about and listening to the latest ideas" (Acts 17:21 NIV). Athens seems to have been full of professional beard-strokers. Picture Gandalf the Wizard in a toga and you're on the right track.

Even for Paul, getting through to the people of Athens was no small task, but his approach can give us insight into how we can be a blessing to places—where we work, our neighborhoods, our communities, and our cities. Paul began by taking the time to listen. He wanted to better understand the people of the place he was trying to reach. So he walked through the city, carefully observing its culture.

> Paul then stood up in the meeting of the Areopagus (the Areopagus was the twenty-four leading philosophers and elders in the city) and said: "People of Athens! I see that in every way you are very religious. For as I walked around and looked carefully at your objects of worship, I even found an altar with this inscription: to an unknown god. So you are ignorant of the very thing you worship—and this is what I am going to proclaim to you." (Acts 17:22–23 NIV)

The Athenians wanted more and more knowledge, so Paul used the fact that they worshipped a god they did *not* know to tell them about the God they *could* know. I love that! Paul listened and observed. And then, when he got an opportunity to speak in the city's most influential forum, he knew what to do.

Listening for the Four P's of a Place

I think Paul's strategy still holds true today. I've heard author Rich Gorman describe it as "listening for the Four 'P's' of a Place." (He later added a fifth P, "Person of Peace," in his ebook *Just Step In: Joining God as He Heals Your City*.) These four "P's of a Place," he says, exist

wherever there are people you can bless, and they can help you know
how to best bless the communities around you. [2]

> The first P is **Pain**. Ask yourself: What are the challenges
> and difficulties that exist in your community? Is it loneli-
> ness, anxiety, addiction? Strained and broken relation-
> ships? There's pain in every place, and if you want to bless
> a particular community, you cannot turn a blind eye to
> its pain.
>
> The second P is **Pennies**—understanding the economy
> of a place. What kinds of jobs make up your community?
> Where is there opportunity for prosperity? How has the local
> economy affected the lives of the people living there, for good
> and for bad?
>
> The third P is **Power**. Whether it's the mayor's office, the
> local school councils, or business owners, every city or neigh-
> borhood has certain people of influence. And if we are going
> to reach our community, it's important to know who holds
> the power.
>
> The final P is **Parties**. Every community has values it
> cherishes and loves to celebrate. So ask, "What do the
> people here honor and celebrate—even long for?" Maybe
> it's friendship? Or for their children to do well in school?
> When you tap into what people celebrate, you discover the
> heartbeat of a neighborhood or community.

When my brother, Jon, first moved to the north side of Chicago,
he and his wife, Lisa, went to a neighborhood association meeting.
They expected to see a lot of people—fifty, maybe seventy-five. They
figured they would go in and out unnoticed. Nope. There were ten
people in the room. As Jon tried to size up the situation, it looked like
the "regulars" were all sitting around a big oval table in the center of

the room. Later, he found out they were the board members. Everyone else sat around the perimeter of the room—Jon, Lisa, and one other couple. They just sat and listened. Then after about an hour it was "open forum" time and all eyes turned to Jon and Lisa.

"I could tell they expected us to say something," Jon told me. "So I said, 'Thanks! Thanks for all you do, and thanks for letting us come tonight and just listen to all you're doing for our neighborhood.' That's all I said. You would have thought I offered to underwrite their next fundraiser. It was clear they were expecting a problem, a complaint, a criticism from the newcomers. And all we did was listen and say, 'Thanks.' I had no idea that simply listening and saying thanks would mean so much to them!"

Listening is one of the most practical ways you can bless the people around you. Paul would have done anything to bless the place called Athens, and one of the ways he did it was to fully listen to the city. In one of his letters, he wrote: "I have become all things to all people so that by all possible means I might save some" (1 Corinthians 9:22 NKJV).

I like how author Dallas Willard puts it: "The first act of love is always the giving of attention."[3]

The places where we live, work, and play are constantly speaking. If you listen, you will hear them. Whether it's a neighborhood association, the school board, chamber of commerce, or city council, just show up and listen for what God wants you to hear.

Jesus heard one man's voice in a huge crowd of people and asked, "What do you want me to do?" The Apostle Paul loved the people of Athens so much that he was first willing to slow down and listen before he spoke. Every day, you come into contact with people nobody seems to care about or who might intimidate you. My prayer is that as you take Jesus's words and actions to heart—and begin to really listen to the people around you—you will see how God wants to use you to bless the people you love and change lives.

We cannot bless the world without listening to people.

Listening Questions

The following is a simple tool to help you learn how to listen. It is a tool that can profoundly change your relationship with your neighbors because it is a list of questions for you to ask about the people where you live, work, and play.

This tool is adapted from a great resource our friends at Ethos Church in Nashville put together. Take some time to prayerfully ask yourself these questions. You can ask these questions on your own, or better yet with other neighbors or a small group. And don't do this just once because the answers will change. Use this tool over and over again as you bless people by listening.

Questions for Where You Live

Q: Do you know your neighbors' names? If not, how can you introduce yourself?

Q: Who in your neighborhood just had a baby? Can you naturally offer something, take a meal (either take-out or something homemade), or a small gift and card?

Q: Who is elderly or disabled? What might they need help with? (Yard work, house chores, caring for a pet, etc.)

Q: Who is around your age or in a similar life stage? Can you invite them into your space or home?

Q: Are there single moms or dads around you? How might they need help from time to time?

Q: Do your neighbors know each other? Can you do something to bring them all together?

Q: Are there other people who follow Jesus in your neighborhood? If so, can you partner together to look for and meet needs?

Q: Do you know of birthdays, anniversaries, or other special events happening? How can you help someone celebrate?

Q: Who has moved in recently? How can you help welcome them to the neighborhood?

Q: Is there anyone in your neighborhood who doesn't fit the profile of the majority? How can you help them feel loved and valued?

Q: Is there someone who lives around you who has served or helped you? Is there a small gesture you can make to show your thanks? (A thank-you card, homemade cookies, etc.)

Questions for Where You Work

Q: Do you know your coworkers' names? If not, how can you introduce yourself?

Q: Has anyone had any major life changes?

Q: Has there been a death in anyone's family, or are they or someone in their family ill?

Q: Has anyone at work just had a baby? Can you naturally offer something, take a meal (either take-out or something homemade), or a small gift and card?

Q: Is there someone at your workplace or school who doesn't fit in, is different, or gets bullied? How can you help them feel loved and valued?

Q: Is there anyone new to your workplace? How can you help them feel welcome?

Q: Are there others in your workplace who follow Jesus or are curious about faith? How can you engage in conversations about faith or let them know you are a follower of Jesus?

Q: Do you know of birthdays, anniversaries, or other special events happening? How can you help someone celebrate?

Q: Do any of your coworkers hang out together after work? How can you join in or initiate a gathering?

Q: Are there ways you can support your coworkers after work? Do you have a coworker who plays in a band or has a hobby that you can support them in?

Q: Is there a coworker who always goes out of their way to help or serve you? How could you acknowledge their kindness or express your thanks?

Questions for Where You Play

Q: Where do you go frequently? (Gym, library, sporting events, music venues, restaurants, cafés, bars, bookstores, recreational leagues?) How can you get to know the people you see frequently at this place?

Q: Can you take opportunities to make a significant encounter something more? It may be the barista, bartender, someone checking you in at the gym, or running beside you on a treadmill.

Q: How can you listen and express care for that person with whom you regularly interact?

Q: How can you do more than simply come in and out of these places undetected, and instead begin to look for small and big ways to appreciate, engage with, and encourage people there?

Q: How can you make this place a better and more positive place?

Q: Is there someone you have favor with? For example, does the manager of the gym, the barista at your café, or the wait staff at your favorite restaurant enjoy talking to you? How can you listen to and bless those people?

In his book *Jesus Is the Question*, Martin P. Copenhaver says that Jesus asked 307 questions and answered only three of them. The rest of the time He just listened. Clearly a part of Jesus's way of loving the people around Him was to ask good questions and then listen. Let's do the same!

I guess about now you may be thinking, *"Begin with Prayer" and "Listen"? I was hoping for something a little more action-oriented, something a little more assertive.* As an extrovert, I understand that feeling. On the other hand, if you lean more toward the introverted side, you're likely thinking, *So far, so good. I can do this!*

Either way, I have a message for you: Don't underestimate the power of beginning with prayer and listening. The remaining three

B.L.E.S.S. practices are more action-oriented and will definitely push you out of your comfort zone. But I promise they won't be effective if you don't first begin with prayer and listen. I am almost certain the next chapter covers what will become your favorite way to bless your neighbors and change the world. It's definitely mine.

B.L.E.S.S. Discussion Questions

OPEN: What is your most memorable "Mondegreen Moment" when you misheard a word or phrase that made sense in your head but was entirely incorrect?

_____

_____

_____

_____

_____

DIG: Why do we have such a difficult time truly listening to the people around us?

_____

_____

_____

_____

_____

Have you ever felt unheard? What was that like for you?

_____

_____

_____

_____

_____

Read Luke 18:35–42. What impresses you most about Jesus's interaction with the man who was blind? How would you have felt if you were that man?

_____

_____

_____

_____

_____

When was the last time you truly felt listened to, known, and loved? What was so special about that experience?

_____

_____

_____

_____

_____

Read Acts 17:21-23. How do you think the people of Athens felt when Paul spoke to them?

_____

_____

_____

_____

_____

REFLECT: Review "Listening to the Four P's of Place: Pain, Pennies, Power, and Parties." Use one of those to describe a community around you.

_____

_____

_____

_____

_____

Choose one area—where you live, work, or play—and answer two or three of the Listening Questions. Record your answers below.

_____

_____

_____

_____

_____

CHAPTER 5

E: Eat

BIG IDEA
To B.L.E.S.S. your neighbors, Jesus invites you
to eat with them.

Lou Malnati's. Portillo's. Ann Sather's. If you've ever lived in Chicago or even just visited, your mouth is probably watering. I have lived in Chicago my whole life. These restaurants are staples in my family's life.

I know I'm biased, but I don't have any problem saying that Chicago is in a class by itself when it comes to restaurants and great food, particularly deep-dish pizza. (I also think the Chicago White Sox are the best, but that's a whole other argument). Bottom line: Chicagoans are proud of our food, and we love it!

I'm sure you have your own list of favorite places to eat. Those are the places everyone in your friend group or family gets excited about. You can probably make a great argument why yours is the "best foodie city." In general, I think Americans have a love affair with food.

Despite all that, we often fail to recognize the power of eating—specifically the experience of eating *with* someone. Something special happens when we gather at the table.

Listening and eating make a great combo!

Some things are just better together, like pea-nut butter and jelly. This is also true of the two practices of listening and eating! Why do these two make such a power-ful one-two punch? First, because neighbors seldom share meals together. In our individualistic society, hospitality is seen as an extravagant gesture of good will. Second, when the focus of the meal is centered on good conversation to get to know your neighbor, it comes across as a tremen-dously generous act. Much of Jesus's ministry involved con-versation around a table. In the book of Luke alone, there are ten stories of Jesus dining and talking with various peo-ple. Active listening coupled with a good meal can catapult a casual acquaintance into a growing friendship.

A Thursday at McDonald's

A few Thanksgivings ago, I heard a story that was going viral on social media. On a Thursday morning, a young African-American man named Eric, wearing baggy jeans and a flat brimmed Black-hawks hat, headed to his local McDonald's to eat breakfast by him-self. Jan, a white seventy-year-old grandmother, had the same idea.

As they were both eating by themselves, Jan saw Eric sitting by himself. She approached him and said, "Could we enjoy our break-fasts together?" Somewhat startled by her request, he reluctantly said, "Sure." And with that, Jan grabbed her food tray and took it over to Eric's table. Eric pulled up a chair so she could sit down.

The two of them sat together for forty-five minutes talking about church, art, and Eric's young son. Eric said Jan even shared some life wisdom with him.

"She mentioned many times how we all should love one another, and how we should never judge anyone because you never know how someone's day is going and what they've been through," he said in an interview. After they finished eating, they exchanged phone numbers, and Eric walked Jan to her car. A simple meal shared with a stranger became a lasting blessing.

This story spread like wildfire. I think it was so loved because stories like this seem so rare; our world longs for the blessing of a shared meal.

But what if these stories weren't so rare? What if we made them common in our communities? What do you think our neighborhoods would look like if our homes and neighborhoods became hubs for expressing the love of Jesus by sharing a meal?

I'm convinced that eating *with* someone is one of the most powerful ways you can bless your neighbors and change the world.

Eating with "Sinners"

Not surprisingly, some of the strongest examples of the power of eating together come from Jesus. Throughout Scripture, we see Him eat with people. But if I asked you to list all the ways Jesus blessed the people around Him during His time on Earth, I'm guessing that eating with people wouldn't be on it.

You would probably mention teaching, healing, doing miracles, praying, walking on water, eventually dying on a cross, and three days later overcoming death and coming back to life. But did you ever notice that part of how Jesus blessed and saved the world was by…wait for it…*eating*? I know it may sound a little crazy, but eating was actually central to Jesus's mission of loving others and showing them God's love!

In fact, much of His ministry centered around meals. He performed His first miracle at a wedding feast (John 2:1–12). One of His most well-known miracles was feeding the five thousand on a hill in the countryside

(John 14:13–21). The night before His crucifixion, He brought together His closest friends for a meal (Luke 22:7–20). And after His resurrection, He shared breakfast on the beach with His disciples (John 21:1–14).

As people who scarf down fast food on the go while steering with our knees, I'm not sure we really grasp how big a deal eating was in Jesus's culture. It was a statement of friendship. It was an affirmation of that person's value, dignity, and worth. Who you ate with indicated who you loved and considered to be part of your social class.

That's why it was so scandalous to the religious leaders that He frequently ate with the lowest and most hated people of the day. Respectable rabbis didn't eat with those who weren't part of the "good people" group.

One of the best examples of this comes from Matthew's report of what happened when Jesus ate with a tax collector. What makes this encounter even more captivating is that the tax collector Matthew was writing about was himself. I love how he tells this story:

> As Jesus went on from there, he saw a man named Matthew sitting at the tax collector's booth. "Follow me," he told him, and Matthew got up and followed him. While Jesus was having dinner at Matthew's house, many tax collectors and "sinners" came and ate with him and his disciples. When the Pharisees saw this, they asked his disciples, "Why does your teacher eat with tax collectors and sinners?" On hearing this, Jesus said, "It is not the healthy who need a doctor, but the sick. But go and learn what this means: 'I desire mercy, not sacrifice. For I have not come to call the righteous, but sinners.'" (Matthew 9:9–13 NIV)

In Jesus's day, tax collectors were considered the scum of the earth. Tax collectors worked for the Roman Empire. Most Jewish people considered them traitors because they made money by overcharging their own people. Tax collectors were seen but rarely spoken to, and certainly not someone you'd share a meal with.

Notice the first thing Jesus did after Matthew said "yes" to following Him wasn't to enroll Matthew in a class on how to be a disciple. He didn't challenge him to start studying the Bible and memorizing Scripture. Those would have been vitally important assignments, but instead, He simply went to Matthew's house to eat.

And who else joins them for this meal? Even more tax collectors, along with a whole group of people referred to as "sinners." The term "sinner" in Jesus's day was a catch-all term for anybody who wasn't religious or who was involved in an illicit lifestyle, like prostitution. The crowd at Matthew's house was a veritable who's who of the socially unacceptable.

In fact, it was so unacceptable that the religious establishment tried to undermine Jesus by asking His disciples, "Why does your teacher eat with tax collectors and 'sinners'?" But Jesus overheard them. I don't know if this is how it happened, but I picture Jesus with a mouthful of chicken, shaking a drumstick at them and saying: "It's not the healthy who need a doctor, but the sick." (To be clear, Jesus was not saying the religious Pharisees were the healthy, good people who didn't need a doctor.)

Then He said, "Go and learn what this means, 'I desire mercy, not sacrifice,'" taking a page from the Old Testament. The Pharisees were famous for knowing the Old Testament backward and forward. They were all-stars at memorization and performing religious rituals and sacrifices, but they ignored the poor and the marginalized. So Jesus said, "You know God says, 'I desire mercy, not sacrifice,' but you don't really know what it means. And if you do, you aren't living it out."

Jesus was on a mission with His life, and the Pharisees didn't get it. For them, the first priority was obedience to laws, but for Jesus it was blessing people. He came to show them grace and mercy. And not just to hope people would find their way back to God, but to help them do it.

Praying for an empty house

The house next door to Brooke and Justin was like a revolving door of new neighbors. Over a five-year span a stream of people rented the house, then just as quickly would disappear and move out. With each new neighbor came the excitement of getting to know them, but that was quickly followed by the letdown of a quick departure.

Then a couple moved in and stayed. Brooke and Justin began to pray for them and looked for an opportunity to connect. But this new couple wasn't interested. They would come home from work and drive into the garage. They wouldn't be seen again until the next morning when the garage door opened and they drove away. An occasional "How are you?" followed by "I'm fine" was as far as the relationship ever got. Then that couple moved too.

Brooke and Justin were frustrated, but they prayed, "God, you know this house is vacant again. Please give us some neighbors we can love and do life with."

Another young couple, Lauren and Quentin, moved in. Brooke and Justin went next door and welcomed them to the neighborhood, intentionally using the practices of B.L.E.S.S. The next week they invited their new neighbors over for a cookout. That meal included a long conversation about jobs, favorite sports teams, and restaurant recommendations. It was a great time.

When Brooke found out their new friends had not yet bought a lawn mower, she "encouraged" Justin to mow their yard when he mowed their own. He continued to do so every week without being asked. It was hard for their new neighbors not to notice that their grass was magically shorter every weekend!

Finally, Lauren asked Brooke, "Tell me. Why are you so different? Why do you seem to always go out of your way to help us out?" Brooke began to share some of her story about Jesus.

Not much later, Lauren came over and said, "I wanted to update you on something."

"Yeah, what's that?" said Brooke.

"Quentin and I decided to stop renting and buy our house. I wanted you to know the biggest reason we bought it was because of the neighbors. Thanks!"

Several weeks later, Quentin crossed the lawn and told Justin, "I just got news that my uncle died suddenly. I'm having some really deep questions about God and what happens after you die. I know you have faith. Could we talk?" The two of them sat down in the front yard for a couple hours, and Justin led Quentin to Christ there. The following Sunday he baptized him, with Brooke and Lauren in church along with them.

Brooke would tell you, "It all started with us praying for that empty house, asking God to give us neighbors we could love. Now they are some of our very best friends."

Matthew, Mark, Luke, and John were diligent about recording how Jesus called out the religious leaders for their criticism. On another occasion he said, "The Son of Man (one of Jesus's favorite ways of referring to Himself) came eating and drinking, and you say, 'Here is a glutton and a drunkard, a friend of tax collectors and sinners'" (Luke 7:34–35 NIV).

Of course, we know Jesus was neither a drunkard nor a glutton, but He so frequently ate with people who were that He was accused of it—a lot. Because for Jesus, eating was essential to His mission of seeking and saving the lost. He blessed and loved people by sharing meals with them.

He Gave Them a Meal

It was around a table in the Upper Room that Jesus used the bread to tell His disciples His body would be beaten, stabbed, bruised, and hung on a tree, and used the wine to represent the blood that would

Get invited over to eat.

The missional practice of eating doesn't have to happen only in your house or on your dime! In fact, it can happen when you get invited to someone else's party and they are paying for it! One of the things I admire about Jesus is that sometimes He hosted dinner for others. How about the time He had more than five thousand guests and fed them all (Matthew 14:13-21)? Seriously, that had to be a good time! And sometimes He got invited to parties, like the one at Levi's house (Luke 5:27-32) or the wedding at Cana (John 2:1-11). And when the wine ran out, He made sure there was more and better wine! (That will get you on a lot of invite lists!) Whether it was dinner at His place or a night on the town, He saw them as missional opportunities. Wherever there was good food and people, there was an opportunity to deepen relationships and make friends. So don't just think you have to have people over to your place; see if you can become the kind of person they invite over to their place!

pour out of Him. It was around a table that Jesus spoke words that have become foundational to us as His followers.

Author and Bible scholar N.T. Wright says, "When Jesus himself wanted to explain to his disciples what his forthcoming death was all about, he didn't give them a theory; he gave them a meal."[1]

Through His sacrifice, Jesus invites us all to share a meal at His table of grace, forgiveness, and blessing. Which means that we too can invite our friends, coworkers, and neighbors to share meals of grace and blessing with us.

But does it really work? Does something as simple as sharing a meal—eating with someone—change lives? Let me tell you one of my favorite stories. It begins with a barbecue grill.

BBQ in the Driveway

Rudy and Amber are a couple at our church who, like many of us, didn't know their neighbors. So they started praying for them and listening to them. Theirs is an extremely diverse neighborhood full of people from different cultures and different life stages. Some are brand-new too; others have been around for years. Rudy and Amber decided that food might be something that could bring this group together, so every Tuesday, they pulled their barbecue grill in front of the house and invited everyone over for a meal.

For the first four weeks, one family showed up—or no one at all, except Rudy and Amber. Then after a month of prayer and consistent grilling, they had a breakthrough, and soon the whole neighborhood was eating together.

Then something else happened: the conversation shifted from the weather to deeper topics. People began to discuss relational and financial struggles. They were becoming friends. They even started serving one another. Rudy and Amber were blessing their neighborhood! Recently, they told me, "We know it's only a matter of time till one of them says 'yes' to Jesus."

I love what author Henri Nouwen wrote about the power of eating together. He said, "When we invite friends for a meal, we do much more than offer them food for their bodies. We offer friendship, fellowship, good conversation, intimacy, and closeness. When we say, 'Help yourself…take some more…don't be shy…have another glass …' we offer our guests not only our food and drink but also ourselves. A spiritual bond grows, and we become food and drink for one another."[2]

Excuses, Excuses

Let me warn you: When you start thinking and praying about blessing your neighbors through this third practice of eating, it will become
very easy and also tempting to come up with all sorts of excuses for
why you can't do it.

Excuse #1: "I don't like to have people in my home."

When we start talking about this practice, some people tell me,
"I'm not much of a cook. I don't like to eat my own food, let alone
ask someone else to eat it." Or "I don't feel good about the way my
house looks; we don't even really have a table." If you don't like to
have people in your home, that's OK. Eat out. If you can't cook, order
in. Don't fall into the trap of thinking you have to prepare an eight-
course meal to invite someone to dinner. Remember, it's not about
what you're eating or even where you're eating it. It's about who you're
eating with.

Here's another common excuse:

Excuse #2: "I wouldn't know what to say."

A lot of us aren't used to entertaining guests. You may be anxious
about what you'd talk about. No one likes awkward silences. Some
people are simply more naturally outgoing than others.

Let me encourage you with this: Eating together provides a great
opportunity to live out what we talked about in the previous chapter—
listening. Instead of worrying about what you'll *say*, think about what
you can *learn* about the other person—by *listening*.

Start conversations with questions like:

- Where did you grow up?
- What kinds of jobs have you had in your career?
- What do you do for fun?
- What are your dreams for the future?

- Where did you meet? (If your neighbors are married or dating)

Take a photo of these questions and keep them on your smartphone for when you need them.

Instead of worrying about having the perfect words to say, focus on just being present, asking questions, and listening to the people God has put in your life. Remember, you've already been praying for and listening to them (the first two practices of B.L.E.S.S.). Trust God on this adventure!

Here's a third excuse that may be the biggest barrier of all:

Excuse #3: "I just don't have time."

Many of us, myself included, can barely find time to eat meals with our own families, let alone with other people, right? I get it. Finding the time to eat with people can seem next to impossible.

Think about it this way: Eating is already on our schedules. In fact, most of us find time to eat at least two and probably three times every day, even when there is a lot of uncertainty in our weeks. If you eat three times a day, that's twenty-one times a week.

I'm not asking you to do anything I don't do. My wife, Sue, and I have become intentional about regularly eating with friends both in our home and at restaurants. I'll be the first to say that it takes some effort. But we've discovered that even on those evenings when we would really rather have a quiet evening at home, we end the evening feeling grateful and thankful we made the effort to share a meal.

The Power of Sharing a Meal

So what would it look like if you set aside just one or two meals (out of twenty-one) every week to bless people by eating with them? Picture a world where people are sitting together, eating, talking, listening, and connecting to one another. I believe that's a picture God is waiting to see!

When you start to practice this simple, everyday way of blessing your neighbors, you might even discover that hospitality is a spiritual gift you didn't know you had. I'm convinced you'll be amazed by how you can impact the lives of people around the table. You're going to find yourself helping others eat their way into the Kingdom of God.

Remember, you don't have to do this alone. I encourage everyone in our church to get into a small group because we believe to our core that we were never meant to pursue the Jesus Mission solo. What if your small group started having barbecues, parties, or dinners once a month, inviting neighbors, coworkers, and friends? What if you skipped the Bible study and decided to just hang out, eat, and party? That could be someone's first taste of your small group, of your church—and of God!

In their book *Right Here, Right Now*, my friends Alan Hirsch and Lance Ford write about what it looks like to live on mission every day. They say that sharing meals together is "one of the most sacred practices we can engage in as believers." They even go as far to say that if every Christian family regularly invited a stranger or a poor person into their home for a meal once a week, we would "literally change the world by eating!"[3]

What if they're right? I think they are. I think Jesus understood this too. If you knew the only thing standing between a neighbor or a friend and eternal life was your eating dinner with them, would you do it? I know you would.

Please don't forget what's at stake here. I know there are many reasons that make eating together difficult and uncomfortable. But I believe it's worth pushing through our excuses and getting out of our comfort zones so we can truly love our neighbors and change the world one meal at a time.

Meal Calendar

This simple tool is another reminder that the B.L.E.S.S. practices are not a program but a new way to live your life. Earlier in this chapter, I said that most of us eat three meals a day, seven days a week. You do not have to do anything different—just use any of the twenty-one opportunities to bless a friend or neighbor by sharing a meal.

Use this simple tool at the beginning of every week to pick just one meal or one coffee (add dessert if you really want to be a blessing!) to bless someone. I'm not asking you to add a single minute to your schedule. I'm simply challenging you to include someone in something you're already doing. But plan it out.

EAT	S	M	T	W	R	F	S
breakfast							
lunch							
dinner							
coffee							

Ten Thousand Taste Buds

I'm becoming increasingly convinced that food is grace from God. Is there any other way to explain why the average human has about ten thousand taste buds? It didn't have to be that way! God didn't have to make us with recurring appetites and the ability to satisfy that appetite with such delight. He could have made us as beings for whom food is just fuel to get us from here to there. Our ten thousand taste buds are a grace from God.

That makes the table a great place to schedule a blessing from God. Perhaps before we invite people to Jesus or invite them to church, we should invite them to dinner!

I have scheduled early breakfasts or coffee to meet with executives who start their days at the crack of dawn. Sue and I have used our fire pit to invite couples over for drinks and dessert late into the evening. We have used dinner out at a favorite restaurant to deepen friendships and as an opportunity to bless others. Use this tool of a meal calendar to experience God's grace and to be a blessing.

Dinner Church

If using this simple tool and hosting a meal once a week for your neighbors goes as well as I anticipate, you could end up planting a new church. Why? Because that is what happened to Verlon Fosner. For the last decade he and his church have been hosting weekly gatherings they call "Dinner Church." Fosner launched Seattle's first Dinner Church more than a decade ago. Since then, six other Dinner Churches have started in that area, with approximately forty Dinner Churches across the country and more coming!

Fosner says, "It's the best metaphor for the Gospel we've found. We put out quality, abundant food because we'd rather show the Gospel than have to just explain it. People walk through the line and see more food than they can possibly eat—all the colors and carved meats—and they realize Jesus paid for this. They're not being billed for it. The food provides a critical, immediate sense of abundance of generosity and divine care for people."

It was at a Dinner Church in the Upper Room that Jesus blessed His friends and followers with an act of service that stunned everyone present—a seismic shift that turned the world on its head. In the next chapter, we'll discover how we can follow His example and make the same kind of impact. I'm not exaggerating. Don't believe me? Read on, and I'll show you.

B.L.E.S.S. DISCUSSION QUESTIONS

OPEN: Pick one to answer:

If you could eat anywhere for dinner, where would you go?

_____

_____

_____

_____

_____

What is your most memorable meal ever?

_____

_____

_____

_____

DIG: Have you ever experienced sharing a meal with some-one, and suddenly that acquaintance became a friend? What is it about sharing a meal that seems to deepen a friendship so quickly?

_____

_____

_____

_____

Read Matthew 9:9–13. Why do you think Jesus chose to eat with Matthew? How do you think Matthew felt about sharing a meal with Jesus?

_____

_____

_____

What point was Jesus making when He said that He "came eating and drinking…" (Luke 7:34 NIV)? What does this say about how He wanted to be known?

_____

_____

_____

_____

Why is eating with someone such an effective way to bless them?

_____

_____

_____

_____

_____

Which of the excuses for not sharing a meal with someone do you relate to most?

_____

_____

_____

_____

_____

REFLECT: Who will you share a meal, dessert, or coffee with this week?

_____

_____

_____

_____

_____

CHAPTER 6

S: Serve

BIG IDEA
To B.L.E.S.S. your neighbor, Jesus invites you to serve.

It was 1894 when a British physicist named Lord Kelvin took the podium at a gathering of physicists called the British Association for the Advancement of Science. (My guess is this event was as stuffy as it sounds.)

By that time, the field of physics had made major strides forward. In fact, science had made so much progress that there was a growing group of physicists who thought they had nearly exhausted its limits. Lord Kelvin was part of that group.

Lord Kelvin confidently made a statement that is now infamous in the world of science. In front of everyone, he boldly said, "There is *nothing* new to be discovered in physics. All that remains is more and more precise measurement."[1]

That was Lord Kelvin thinking he dropped the mic, when actually he dropped the ball!

Eleven years later, a wild-haired, bespectacled German genius named Albert Einstein burst onto the scene. (Something about Albert's appearance makes me think he wasn't invited to the British tea party for science.)

What if you let them serve you?

A counselor once told me, "Dave, if you really want to make good friends with someone, ask them to do something for you." Sounds counterintuitive, doesn't it? However, that is exactly what Jesus told His disciples to do. When He sent them out in pairs, He told them to look for a "person of peace" (Luke 10:6). Then He explained this person was someone who welcomes you and gives you lodging; someone who feeds you; someone who opens up their relational world to you. Jesus said, "When you find that person, stay with them!" That is a great place to start your mission. We tend to think that service starts with our going out and doing things for other people—and it often does. But sometimes, as with Jesus's disciples, it starts with letting them serve you.

Einstein published a paper on "Special Relativity" that turned *everything* physicists—including Lord Kelvin—were certain of on its head. I don't know enough about physics to explain it, but I do know that Einstein's work literally changed the way we understand our world. For two hundred years, physics had been traveling in one direction. After Einstein's paper, everyone had to turn around and walk the opposite way.

It was a seismic paradigm shift that forever changed the field of science. That's what paradigm shifts do; they change the way you see the world.

A Crown for an Apron

Scripture records several world-changing shifts. One was Jesus's last encounter with His closest followers prior to the crucifixion, just before

He shared the Passover meal with His closest friends. Jesus knew He would be arrested that night—and that the next day, He'd be put to death. What He did that evening in the Upper Room represented a shift that overturned a lie that had plagued humanity since the Garden of Eden—the lie that says if you want to be blessed, look out for yourself before anyone else.

Jesus knew His position and power. He knew that God had put all things under His authority. And yet what did He do? I would say He set aside His crown for an apron. The one who sat in the highest position stooped down to serve.

So far we've talked about the first three ways to love your neighbor and change the world: Begin with Prayer, Listen, and Eat. In this chapter I want to talk about the fourth B.L.E.S.S. practice, and that is to Serve. Jesus told us pointedly, "[T]he Son of Man did not come to be served, but to serve…" (Matthew 20:28 NIV). He modeled for us that once you begin with prayer, listen, and eat with someone, there is a good chance that by then you'll have discovered how you can best serve the person God is asking you to bless.

John, Jesus's close friend and disciple, records the scene this way:

> Jesus knew that the Father had put all things under his power, and that he had come from God and was returning to God; so he got up from the meal, took off his outer clothing, and wrapped a towel around his waist. After that, he poured water into a basin and began to wash his disciples' feet, drying them with the towel that was wrapped around him. (John 13:3–5 NIV)

I want you to understand the magnitude of what's happening here. Jesus is God in the flesh, the Maker and Sustainer of everything, the King of kings and Lord of lords. There is no one higher, no one with more power. Even if you were in the room and didn't fully understand

His cosmic authority, you would still have known Him as a highly respected teacher and rabbi.

In the ancient world, washing someone's feet was a routine practice before sharing a meal. But it was a job for the lowest-ranking person in the house. And I doubt I have to tell you it was a gross job!

In the first century, the feet were two of the dirtiest areas of the body. Just imagine no nail clippers, no pedicures, no socks, and a culture where shoes were seldom worn. In this agrarian culture, it was almost impossible to avoid stepping into "stuff" that would make feet truly disgusting!

For a meal like this, Jesus's friends would have reclined at a table and sat on the floor. All those gross, gnarly feet might even be within inches of your face. Just imagine the awkward silence in the room as the disciples realized there was no servant to wash their feet.

Now if I were there, I hate to admit it, but I would have put what my wife calls my "task-avoidance skills" to work! I would've pretended not to notice the dirty feet, maybe feigned a slight injury like a back problem or a headache. That usually works at home. But then the awkwardness meter gets dialed up to eleven as Jesus, the disciples' teacher and rabbi, their Lord, takes His shirt off, ties an apron around His waist, and starts to wash the feet of His followers.

Keep in mind that theirs was an honor-and-shame culture. Protecting your reputation and your dignity was critically important. Your honor was like your credit rating: the higher your honor score, the more privilege and prestige you enjoyed. If you had a high honor score, other people were expected to serve you. Washing feet in public would be a great way to tank your honor score. No one would risk that!

It's why Peter responds to Jesus this way:

> He came to Simon Peter, who said to him, "Lord, are you going to wash my feet?" Jesus replied, "You do not realize now what I am doing, but later you will understand." "No," said Peter, "you shall never wash my feet." (John 13:8a NIV)

Maybe this will help you grasp the significance of what's happening here: Think of someone well beyond you in wealth, status, and fame. Imagine LeBron James coming to your house for dinner. Even if you, like me, know that Michael Jordan is the GOAT (greatest of all time), you still might be a little anxious about having King James in your home, right? And at the same time, you're also honored. Then imagine if after the meal, he gets up, goes to your bathroom, and starts scrubbing your toilet. Wouldn't that make you uncomfortable?

I think that's how Peter felt—times a thousand! So how does Jesus respond?

> Jesus answered, "Unless I wash you, you have no part with me." "Then, Lord," Simon Peter replied, "not just my feet but my hands and my head as well!" (John 13:8b–9 NIV)

Peter didn't realize what Jesus was doing. In just a few hours, Jesus would choose to be stripped and humiliated. His crown would again be set aside, but not for an apron—this time, it would be for a cross. He would take on the full weight of our sins and wash us once and for all with His grace so that we could be clean forever and restored to a right relationship with God.

Jesus washes feet. And what I want to drive home here is this: What Jesus did in the Upper Room the night before His crucifixion was not just a kind gesture; it was meant to catalyze a movement. This was a seismic paradigm shift.

The story continues:

> When he had finished washing their feet, he put on his clothes and returned to his place. "Do you understand what I have done for you?" he asked them. "You call me 'Teacher' and 'Lord,' and rightly so, for that is what I am. Now that I, your Lord and Teacher, have washed your feet, you also

should wash one another's feet. I have set you an example
that you should do as I have done for you. Very truly I tell
you, no servant is greater than his master, nor is a messen-
ger greater than the one who sent him. Now that you know
these things, you will be blessed if you do them." (John
13:12–17 NIV)

Jesus's message is simple: It's now our turn to serve the way Jesus
served. It's your turn to set aside your crown for an apron. We live
in a world that believes the higher you rise and the more power and
wealth you accumulate, the more leverage you have to get others to
serve *you*. But Jesus takes that idea and says, "Here is what it really
looks like to bless the world: you serve!"

Taking Out the Trash

Some of us tend to avoid even the simplest tasks that might be
associated with serving. My brother, Jon, tells the following funny
story that I bet anyone who is married can relate to.

"When Lisa and I got married, we agreed it was my responsibility
to take out the trash. While I did agree to this, I'm not sure I knew
what I was saying 'yes' to back then. I didn't know it meant I had
exclusive rights (a binding contract) for trash-hauling and that no
one else would ever take out the trash. We have two kids, and on
occasion I would go out of town for a few days, come home, and not
only would the trash can be full, but refuse would be piling up on
the floor around it. Sometimes I would just leave it there to see if
anybody would notice. And guess what? Nobody did. Even worse,
when I did take it out, I'd get nothing for my efforts: No recognition.
No accolades. No thanks. It was like nobody ever noticed my selfless
and sacrificial service. About the same time Lisa and I decided I was
the garbage man, we also decided that she would be the laundry girl.

Serving alongside your neighbor works!

Serving together can be a tremendously bonding experience. The missional practice of serving doesn't have to be only you serving your neighbor; it can also be you and your neighbor serving alongside each other. After a bad flood in our city, my wife and I, along with several of our neighbors, came together to help those whose homes were damaged. I felt a special connection with the neighbors we were serving, but I couldn't help but notice I also felt a unique connection with the neighbors I was serving alongside. Look for opportunities to serve your community (food collection, P.A.D.S., Habitat for Humanity, etc.) and invite your neighbors to join you. Coming together during a shared crisis or helping someone else in need can be a catalyst for creating a strong friendship.

I will admit that laundry is a bigger job than the trash. Sometimes I would walk by the laundry room and it would appear that things were a little backed up with clothes spilling out of the laundry basket and onto the floor. Do you think I picked them up? No! Not if I wasn't getting any help with the trash! (Pretty mature of me, huh?) Yes, I am the guy who lets the laundry pile up and the garbage overflow. And too often I look the other way when there's an opportunity to serve."

I bet Jon is not the only one. Me too. Just ask Sue! And if you and I hope to bless the people God has put in our lives, we're going to have to make a major shift when it comes to serving others.

Let's take a look at another example of how Jesus served. This time, Mark, a follower of Jesus, tells the story.

Serving a Deaf Man

Mark records a number of encounters Jesus had with people He met as He traveled. One of the most intriguing is Jesus's healing of a deaf man near the Sea of Galilee. Here's what Mark says:

> Again he departed from the borders of Tyre and Sidon, and came to the sea of Galilee, through the midst of the region of Decapolis. They brought to him one who was deaf and had an impediment in his speech. They begged him to lay his hand on him. He took him aside from the multitude, privately, and put his fingers into his ears, and he spat, and touched his tongue. Looking up to heaven, he sighed, and said to him, "Ephphatha!" that is, "Be opened!" Immediately his ears were opened, and the impediment of his tongue was released, and he spoke clearly. He commanded them that they should tell no one, but the more he commanded them, so much the more widely they proclaimed it. They were astonished beyond measure. (Mark 7:31–37 NKJV)

This story offers us three specific lessons about serving others.

Proximity

The first lesson relates to *proximity*. Notice whom Jesus served. Verse 32 says, "They brought to him one who was deaf and had an impediment in his speech. They begged him to lay his hand on him." The people Jesus served were those in front of Him, near Him—those in close proximity. Too often when it comes to serving, we want to do something big and bold. We might not say it out loud, but if we're honest, wouldn't we prefer to do something that gets a little attention?

I can imagine the look in your eyes if I were to ask, "What about doing that for your neighbor?" The look that says, "Nobody ever got a Nobel Peace Prize for loving their neighbor." But what better place to start than with the people near us? How about the people living under your roof? Our mission lies wherever our feet take us. We start with where we live, where we work, where we play, where we hang out, and in our neighborhood. Those are the people we serve!

Now there are some exceptions. Back up to the beginning of verse 31: "Again, he departed from the borders of Tyre and Sidon, and came to the Sea of Galilee, through the midst of the region of Decapolis." God sent Jesus from Tyre and Sidon all the way to the region of the Decapolis (approximately eighty miles). Why? So Jesus could be in close proximity to the people His Father wanted Him to serve.

So when it comes to serving: God has either *sent* you to the people you are to serve or He is *going* to send you to the people you are to serve. Almost without exception, the people you're meant to serve will be in close proximity. Right around you! Who is that in your path? Take a moment and let God bring someone to mind. Think about the eight neighbors you identified from Chapter 3. Got it?

Personally

The next quality I want you to notice is how Jesus served this man *personally*. Verse 33 tells us that Jesus "took him aside," away from the attention of the crowd. Generally, when somebody takes you aside, it's not a good thing, right? As a kid, I can remember my parents taking me aside and giving me the "I brought you into this world and I can take you out" talk. Today, if I see my wife trying to pull me aside, I know I'm in trouble. But Jesus took this guy aside not to discipline him, but to serve him. Why would He do that this time? He healed lots of people publicly before this.

This is my favorite part of this story. Mark says the man was deaf and had a severe speech impediment. He knew what it was like to be made fun of, to feel like a spectacle. Just imagine how he might have been mocked and laughed at as a child. Every time he tried to speak with all sorts of hesitation and fractured words, he drew attention to

"Football" and faith

 After Jesus and his family, Matt loves soccer more than anything. So when he saw a neighbor, Gonzalo, wearing a Manchester United jersey, he immediately struck up a conversation about "football." It turned out that Gonzalo loved European soccer almost as much as Matt. Because they lived in a big city, there were bars that opened early in the morning just to show European soccer matches starting at 6 a.m. Over breakfast in a local pub while cheering for "Man U," Matt and Gonzalo became friends. Matt had been taught the B.L.E.S.S. practices, and since they were already eating together it was easy to apply them in his new friendship with Gonzalo. He then backed up and started praying for Gonzalo too.

Matt's wife, Laura, and Gonzalo's wife, Hilda, hit it off, and soon Matt was connecting Gonzalo and his family with other believers in their friendship circle. Matt wanted Gonzalo to see a genuine faith not only in his own life, but also in the lives of others. Matt found small ways to serve Gonzalo, including giving him some guidance with how to raise his two little girls based on his experience with his own son and daughter. But the most significant way came when Gonzalo lost his job. Over scrambled eggs and soccer at their favorite hangout, Gonzalo confided that he was worried about the future and anxious about his finances. Matt, who owns his own business and is good with money, gave him solid advice. The next morning, Matt told Gonzalo he should apply for a job with his company. Three weeks later, Gonzalo was hired.

Over the next few months Matt would ask Gonzalo if he had any interest in reading Scripture with him and a couple other guys. Gonzalo, who had a nominal Catholic memory from childhood, told him, "No. Everything I remember about the Bible was boring, and I've also heard there is a lot of crazy stuff in there." Matt didn't push back.

Matt doesn't know what changed Gonzalo's mind, but one day, out of the blue, he asked, "You still meeting with those guys at the donut shop and reading the Bible? If so, I might be up for that!" Gonzalo had never read the Bible and was surprised to find out that the stories about David and Goliath and others he'd heard of were actually there. "A lot of this is really confusing, but the stuff about Jesus I'm really interested in!" he said. While he didn't buy into everything in the Bible, Gonzalo was attracted to Jesus.

One morning at Dunkin' Donuts, Gonzalo and the guys were reading in 1 Corinthians about sexual immorality. Gonzalo asked, "So, does this mean that watching pornography is bad?" It had never occurred to him that porn might be personally addictive or bad for his marriage. Without judgment, the guys explained God's vision for lust-free living.

Several weeks later, Gonzalo showed up for coffee, donuts, and Scripture, saying, "Hey, I want you to know that it has been five weeks that I have not watched any pornography." The group congratulated him and shared some of their own struggles and victories.

Gonzalo has not yet come to a place of trust in Jesus, but he's definitely moving in that direction. God's Spirit is at work in his life, and He's using Matt, the B.L.E.S.S. practices, and soccer to draw Gonzalo to Jesus.

his disability. Jesus realized this man's particular challenge and refused to make a spectacle of his condition. He served him with dignity and in a way that showed He understood his needs beyond the obvious ones.

Powerfully

Jesus served in close proximity. He served personally. And lastly, Jesus served powerfully. Don't just run past the big event of this story, thinking it doesn't apply to you. Mark writes, "Looking up to heaven, he sighed, and said to him, 'Ephphatha!' that is, 'Be opened!' Immediately his ears were opened, and the impediment of his tongue was released, and he spoke clearly."

When Jesus served, He accessed God's power. And to me, that is world-changing. Because we can access that same power! When you think about serving, you likely think of doing good deeds—anything from shoveling a driveway to adopting a child. But never forget that when you serve, you have available to you the power of God. Don't believe me? Maybe you'll believe Jesus. In John, He tells His followers (that's you and me), "Very truly I tell you, whoever believes in me will do the works I have been doing, and they will do even greater things than these" (John 14:12 NIV).

So let me remind you, before you read any further, that when you are serving people, if they are sick, pray and ask God to heal them. If they have an addiction, ask God to free them. If they are in a relationship that is hopeless, ask God to reconcile them. You have access to a powerful God.

"Your God Must Be Real!"

I always think about my friend Adam when I talk about B.L.E.S.S.ing people. Adam works in a local retail store. It's definitely not his dream job, but he needed work, so he took it. Adam asked God to use him in that store to bless the people around him. And just as we've been encouraging you, he began by praying for the people he worked with.

After a while, he got to know Jeremy, his boss, and they quickly became friends. Jeremy made it clear he was not a Christ-follower. But because of their growing friendship, he willingly engaged in conversations about God, spirituality, or "religion" as he called it.

As Adam and Jeremy got to know each other better, my friend learned that his boss was a single parent whose son had chronic health problems. One day, Adam noticed Jeremy seemed unusually down.

"Is something wrong?" he asked.

Jeremy told him, "Yeah, it's my son. He's broken out in severe hives and the doctor can't do anything about it. Since I can't send him to school, he's at home by himself, and I'm really worried."

Adam wasn't sure how his boss would react, but he courageously asked, "Do you mind if I pray and ask God to heal him?" To Adam's surprise, without even pausing, Jeremy said, "Sure, go ahead! Please do!"

The store is always busy and full of people, so Adam looked around for a quiet place to pray and ended up in the bathroom by himself. Adam simply prayed, "God, you know I love this guy, and he's hurting because of his son. I know what You can do, so please heal Jeremy's son. Please take away his hives."

After he finished praying, Adam headed back out to the sales floor. Just moments later, he saw his boss running across the room toward him with an astonished look on his face.

"That prayer thing? It really works!" Jeremy said. "Your God must be real because my son just texted me two minutes ago and said 'Dad, you'd never believe it! All my hives are gone!'"

Did you catch that? A guy who's not a believer said, "Your God must be real!" Why? Because he saw the power of God at work! Never forget to access the power of God as you serve others.

Serving "as You Go"

Of course, sometimes serving is doing something as simple as clipping someone's toenails. Let me explain, or rather introduce you to my Grandma Nellie (a.k.a. "GiGi" to her grandkids). GiGi was a proud woman. She lived through the Great Depression and World War II. My grandpa was a hard-working farmer who died way too young from emphysema. So she lived on her own for about thirty years. I remember seeing her teach herself to play the piano in her sixties and learn to ride a bike for the first time when she was almost seventy. She was a strong and determined woman.

But what I grew to admire about her more than anything else was how she served. She lived in the same neighborhood for years, and she blessed that neighborhood in the most loving ways.

Across the street was a neighbor who was actually quite a bit younger than GiGi, but whose health was in serious decline. She was rather large. Somehow (probably through praying, listening, and eating), GiGi discovered that her friend couldn't keep her toenails clipped. (The truth is that she was just too large to reach them.) So my grandma offered to clip her toenails every week.

As you can imagine, this woman was reluctant at first, but GiGi persisted, and eventually her friend agreed. I never saw it happen, but I have a picture in my mind of my eighty-five-year-old Grandma Nellie laying down her pride every week and walking across the street to cut her friend's toenails—and like Jesus did with the deaf man when He served him personally, bringing dignity to her situation.

Serving is an "as you go" sort of activity. It's about a posture of willingness that stands ready to grab an apron (or some toenail clippers) when the opportunity presents itself.

What Do You Need to Put Down?

Let me ask you: What do you need to put down to bless someone through serving them? What is your crown? Is it your time? Your pride? Your convenience?

What would it look like for you to put down your crown and put on an apron where you live? In your neighborhood? In your apartment or condo building?

What would it look like for you to put down your crown and put on an apron at home? With your spouse? Your children? Your

R-P-M-S

The B.L.E.S.S. practices are intentionally sequenced in an order that builds a bond of friendship and helps people feel loved. It's what Jesus did, and it's hard to improve on that. It is in the context of friendship and love that others will often confide in you how you can serve them. For example, in Chapter 2 I told you about my friend Michael who told me about a tragic event from twenty years prior that haunted him every day. He was looking for forgiveness from the tragedy he had caused. I was able to serve him by telling him how he could be forgiven and how God redeems our pain. Other times, people are not as forward with what they need and how you can serve them. That is where this simple tool of R-P-M-S can help you discern how to serve your neighbor.

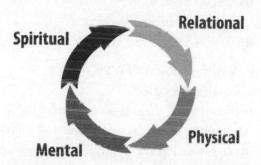

Just as RPMs (revolutions per minute) can help you gauge the health of an engine or motor, I have used a similar acrostic as a way to monitor my own personal well-being for many years. It comes from Luke 2:52, which describes Jesus's own personal development: "Jesus grew in wisdom and stature, and in favor with God and men" (NIV). He grew in these four areas:

Relational: He grew in favor with men.
Physical: He grew in stature.
Mental: He grew in wisdom by developing His mental capacity.
Spiritual: He grew in favor with God.

Every morning I write these four letters (R-P-M-S) at the top of my journal and give myself a score from one to ten on how I'm doing on each of them. I call it a "two-minute checkup." It has been a great help to me personally.

More recently, I've used R-P-M-S to find out how the neighbors and friends I want to bless are doing. Let me briefly give you a few questions to ask about the neighbors you love.

How's my neighbor doing RELATIONALLY?
- How is their home life?
- How is their marriage, dating, or family life going?
- Do they have close friends?
- How are their relationships at work?
- Do they have a healthy circle of friends?

How's my neighbor doing PHYSICALLY?
- How is their overall health?
- Does their energy level seem good?
- Are they getting regular exercise?
- Are their eating habits healthy?
- Do they mention not being able to sleep?

How's my neighbor doing MENTALLY?
- Are there any signs of anxiety?
- Is there any indication of depression?
- Have I noticed any mood swings?
- Are they learning?
- Are there any unhealthy thought patterns showing up?

How's my neighbor doing SPIRITUALLY?
- Do they sense something is missing in their life?
- Are they willing to have you pray for them?
- Do they display a spiritual curiosity?
- Do they initiate spiritual conversations?
- Are they moving closer to God?

Just as we serve ourselves and God when we monitor our personal R-P-M-S, we can bless others in these same four areas. Once you identify their needs, serve them!

---

roommate? Your boss or coworkers? These everyday ways to love your neighbor and change the world aren't just for somebody somewhere; you can start with the people you interact with every single day.

What would it look like for your small group or church to become a community of people who are simply willing to serve?

I'm convinced that when you begin with prayer, listen, and share meals with people, more opportunities to serve than you can count will present themselves! Eventually, someone might even ask you what makes you different or why you serve the way you do. Then you can put into action the fifth and final B.L.E.S.S. practice we'll be talking about in the next chapter. Keep reading. I can't wait for you to see how Jesus drops the mic!

B.L.E.S.S. DISCUSSION QUESTIONS

OPEN: What would you say is the greatest change or paradigm shift of your lifetime?

_____

_____

DIG: Why do we resist serving even the people we care about most?

_____

_____

_____

_____

Read John 13:1-17. Why did Jesus choose to wash His disciples' feet the night before His crucifixion? How would you have felt if you had been there?

_____

_____

_____

_____

_____

Read Mark 7:31-37. What stands out to you about this encounter between Jesus and the deaf man with the speech impediment?

_____

_____

_____

_____

Jesus served in *proximity*, He served *personally*, and He served *powerfully*. Which of these qualities is most difficult for you to exhibit when it comes to serving the people around you?

_____

_____

_____

_____

_____

_____

_____

REFLECT: Who do you think God wants you to serve this week?

_____

_____

_____

_____

_____

_____

_____

Use R-P-M-S to describe some ways you will begin serving the
people God is calling you to serve.

_____

_____

_____

_____

_____

CHAPTER 7

S: Story

BIG IDEA
To B.L.E.S.S. your neighbors, Jesus invites you
to share your story.

Jon and I have spent our whole lives together. As kids, we shared a bunk bed and a trundle bed. (Anyone remember those?) In grade school, we started a lawn-mowing business together—D & J Lawn Mowing! We not only went to the same college, but we were roommates (again). After college graduation we started a church, and we have now worked together for over three decades.

Because of our history, we can look across a room without saying a word and know exactly what the other is thinking! It's an awesome, unfair advantage we have in meetings. I love that when God created us, He designed us with an incredibly complex set of tools for communicating with each other—even without words.

Our faces and body language tell people so much. A smile communicates friendliness, approval, or happiness. A roll of the eye quickly says, "What were you thinking?" A high-five means, "I'm on your side," while a hug or a gentle pat on the back can be the healing touch we need. Teachers will tell you that slouching in your seat says, "I'm not interested at all in what you're telling me," while sitting on the edge of your chair

All great stories are the same.

Storytelling is an art. Every great story has characters, a setting, a plot, a conflict, and a resolution. The character is who the story is about. The setting is the place where it happens. The plot is the beginning, middle, and end of the story. Conflict is the problem in the story, and the resolution is how the problem gets worked out. Without these elements, our stories can become rambling, disconnected, and uninteresting. By simply telling your story in the three parts we suggest—who you were before you met Jesus, how you met Jesus, and what your life has been like since you met Jesus—you will include all five components of a great story and share yours in a way that is clear, concise, and compelling.

and leaning forward usually means, "I'm listening or at least trying to show I'm engaged enough to eke out that A- when I deserve a B+."

There are a myriad of ways we communicate without words, and when it comes to loving our neighbors and reaching people who are far from God, that's exactly how most of us hope we can do it: without words!

It's true, isn't it?

It's why we gravitate to the classic saying I referred to in Chapter 1: "Preach the Gospel at all times. When necessary use words."

Can we really bless our neighbors and friends and change the world without words?

That's what we're talking about in this chapter: our words—or more specifically, our stories.

My hunch is that you could quickly get on board with the first four B.L.E.S.S. practices we discussed. Yes, they require some intention and effort, but they aren't particularly difficult to carry out. For the most part, they don't push you too far out of your comfort zone. However, this final "S" makes many well-intentioned Christians nervous or reluctant to move forward. But you can't spell "B.L.E.S.S." with just one S. And you won't likely help anyone discover the love of God without using your words—and your story.

Jesus Shares His Story

With this fifth B.L.E.S.S. practice, I'm not asking you to do anything I haven't done. Better yet, I'm not asking you to do anything Jesus didn't do Himself—repeatedly. Remember the Pharisee Nicodemus?

"Now a certain man, a Pharisee named Nicodemus, who was a member of the Jewish ruling council, came to Jesus at night..." (John 3:1 NET).

Before we go any further, let me give you the backstory. Nicodemus was part of the group of haughty religious leaders we talked about in Chapter 2—the same group that accused Jesus of being a drunkard and a glutton because He ate with sinners. They were what my grandma would've called "know-it-alls." They were a well-educated and influential group, and as you can tell, they were anti-Jesus all the way—which is why Nicodemus went to talk with Jesus at night. Something about His story had piqued Nicodemus's interest, but he wasn't about to get caught actually talking to Him. So Nicodemus kept his interest in Jesus on the "down low."

> He went to Jesus and said, "Rabbi, we know that you are a teacher who has come from God. For no one could perform the miraculous signs that you do unless God is with him." Jesus replied, "I tell you the solemn truth, unless a person is born from above, he cannot see the kingdom of God." (John 3:1–2 NET)

The conversation starts out with Nicodemus acknowledging that Jesus is from God because of the miracles He'd done. Notice Jesus doesn't say, "Well, thank you very much, Nicodemus. It's great to hear you say that." Instead, Jesus takes the conversation in a very personal direction. He tells Nicodemus he needs to be "born from above."

This concept is difficult for Nicodemus to believe. He had always been taught that everything was fine between him and God. After all, he was an Israelite by birth and obeyed the religious rules.

Yet Nicodemus is curious, so he asks Jesus,

> "How can a man be born when he is old? He cannot be born a second time, can he?" Jesus answered, "I tell you the solemn truth, unless a person is born of water (like a mother's water breaking when the baby's born) and Spirit, he cannot enter the kingdom of God...." Nicodemus replied, "How can these things be?" (John 3:4–5, 9 NET)

Nicodemus seems to be genuinely intrigued by what he's hearing. Jesus is turning his world upside down about what it means to know God. He goes on to ask Nicodemus telling questions and then starts sharing His story. This is where it gets good:

> No one has ascended into heaven except the one who descended from heaven—the Son of Man. (John 3:10–13 NET)

Whoa! Jesus has just said that He's from Heaven—and if you know anything about the Old Testament and what "Son of Man" means (check out Daniel 7), He's just said He's God in the flesh. As a scholar of the scriptures, Nicodemus would've gotten this message loud and clear.

Tell yourself a good news story.

Sharing the story of how Jesus changed your life with a trusted friend who is spiritually searching is very powerful. The stronger the relationship with your friend, the more relevant and powerful your story becomes. But your story can also be a tremendous force in your own life. I've heard it referred to as "telling the Gospel to yourself." Being a follower of Jesus means moving from unbelief to belief in every area of our lives. All of us have areas where we still live in disbelief. One of the best things we can do is to tell the Gospel to ourselves. Recall how good and faithful God has been to you and apply that to areas of disobedience and disbelief. Remember how the grace and goodness of Jesus changed your past, present, and future. Yes, your story can change the lives of others—but it can also change your own!

But Jesus is not done; He continues this eternity altering conversation, sharing more of His story:

So must the Son of Man be lifted up, so that everyone who believes in him may have eternal life. For this is the way God loved the world: He gave his one and only Son, so that everyone who believes in him will not perish but have eternal life. For God did not send his Son into the world to condemn the world, but that the world should be saved through him. (John 3:14–17 NET)

Here, He foreshadows His death and even says why He has to die. Then He just drops the mic: "For God so loved the world that he gave his one and only Son, that whoever believes in him shall not perish but have eternal life" (John 3:16 NIV).

Now that's how you tell a story! Nicodemus comes to Jesus in the middle of the night with a red-hot spiritual interest. Jesus knows this is a time when it's necessary to use words. So He shares the story of who He is, what He's about, and what Nicodemus can do if he wants to find God and experience eternal life. Sounds easy enough, right?

Why Are We Reluctant to Share Our Stories?

If we're going to bless others and share the good news of Jesus, there will be times when words *are* necessary. There's just no getting around it. And yet, most of us hold back, even when we know we have the opportunity to say something that could make a difference.

Have you ever had the feeling that you *should* say something? You know, that moment in a conversation when you get that fluttery feeling in the pit of your stomach, or you hear that voice inside your head that says, *This is it!* I have. At times, I've acted on it. Other times, I haven't. Even though the words were on the tip of my tongue, I stopped myself. Then before I knew it, the opportunity was gone!

Why did I hesitate? And why do *we* often hold back from sharing *our* story?

Reluctant Reason #1: "I just don't have what it takes."

Maybe you've bought into the lie that says, "I just don't have what it takes." So many people think sharing their story is only for super-religious people who understand the Bible backward and forward. After all, what if a debate breaks out or someone asks a question you can't answer?

Just the other night, I was at dinner with a new friend who's not a Christian, and he asked me: "So, Dave, why *did* God put the forbidden fruit in the garden?" He completely caught me off guard. I thought we were just having a casual dinner.

I found myself sweating it out for a few seconds as I choked down the last bite of strip steak. I said a quick prayer, began to fake a cough, and excused myself to the restroom so I could ask someone I knew I could count on: "Siri, why did God put the forbidden fruit in the garden?"

I'm kidding. I thought I answered OK. I'd give my response a B-. But I don't think my friend was really looking for the right answer. I think he just wanted to see if I was willing to have an open and honest conversation.

If you remember just one truth from this entire chapter, let it be this one: You will *not* have all the answers to people's most challenging questions. Let me say that again, because I really want you to get this: You will NOT have all the answers to people's most challenging questions. But what you do have is better—you have the Spirit of God! When Jesus sent His disciples out to share His good news, He said to them: "[D]on't worry about how to respond or what to say. God will give you the right words at the right time. For it is not you who will be speaking—it will be the Spirit of your Father speaking through you" (Matthew 10:19b–20 NLT). Let that sink in!

Somebody once told me, "Good news is better than good arguments." When you use your words to share the love of Jesus with your friends and neighbors, you aren't speaking the good news on your own. If you're following Jesus, you have the Spirit of God living inside you. You actually do have what it takes!

Reluctant Reason #2: "I don't want to impose my beliefs on my friends and family."

You've likely seen the stereotypes, whether in movies, on the evening news, or social media. It's those angry Christians with real or digital bullhorns trying to jam the Bible down people's throats. If that's what you're afraid of, good! Be afraid—and DON'T DO THAT!

Humbly sharing the difference that following Jesus has made in your life is not imposing your beliefs on anyone. I love this classic quote from missiologist D. T. Niles, because it reminds me of what I'm really doing when I share my story:

"Christianity is one beggar telling another beggar where he found bread."[1]

If you believe what you've found in Jesus is good news—the most life-changing, eternity-altering news you could ever share—then why *wouldn't* you use your words to tell others about it? To keep it to yourself would be like hoarding bread when others are going hungry.

In his letter to the Romans, Paul writes, "Everyone who calls on the name of the Lord will be saved" (Romans 10:13 NLT).

But then he goes on to ask:

> But how can they call on him to save them unless they believe in him? And how can they believe in him if they have never heard about him? And how can they hear about him unless someone tells them? (Romans 10:14 NLT)

Do this. Read this verse again, but this time swap out the word "someone" for your own name: "And how can they hear about him unless (your name here) tells them?"

Friend, what you say—yes, your words—can help point people desperate for food to life-saving bread. Your story is compelling (not imposing) because it's *your* story of how *you* found the love of God in Jesus.

Reluctant Reason #3: "Sharing my story makes me feel uncomfortable."

Yes, you might feel uncomfortable telling your story! I get that. You might even get nervous or lose your train of thought. You could stumble over your words. But I gotta cut to the chase: Are you really going to let your feelings stop you from sharing words that could mean the difference in the life and eternity of your friend?

While the discomfort is real, the nervousness and awkwardness you experience is so worth it when you consider the impact and significance. And remember, sharing your story doesn't have to be complicated. Let me show you what I mean.

I Was Blind but Now I See

In John 9, one of Jesus's closest friends and disciples tells us about a guy who simply shared his life-changing story with his neighbors. "As Jesus was walking along, he saw a man who had been blind from birth" (John 9:1 NET).

We don't know this man's name. We only know that he's blind and has been all his life. Then a little later, John tells us he's "the man who used to sit and beg" (John 9:8 NIV).

So not only is he blind, but he's also a beggar. As Jesus comes across this man, He does a very strange thing. He spits on the ground, makes mud from it, and spreads the mud over the blind beggar's eyes.

If this were my story, I'm not sure I would've loved the idea of someone spreading spit-filled mud on my eyes. But the blind man cooperates and follows Jesus's next instructions to wash out his eyes. Then look what happens: "So the man went and washed and came back seeing" (John 9:7 NIV)!

A miracle!

This man who had been blind since birth suddenly can see! Can you even imagine? For years you've lived in utter darkness, and in a matter of minutes Jesus smears mud over your eyes, and *voila!* You can see clear as day.

Obviously, the guy is completely blown away—and he can't keep quiet. When his neighbors ask him what happened, he says:

The man they call Jesus made mud and spread it over my eyes and told me, "Go to the pool of Siloam and wash yourself." So I went and washed, and now I can see! (John 9:11 NIV)

Notice that this man can't fully explain how it happened. And I'm guessing he was a little hesitant to share about the spitting part, so he simply tells them what Jesus did and how his life is now forever changed.

What I love about this story is that we can't always explain exactly what happened after we chose to follow Jesus either. We just know it happened. And that's OK. Later, when the man is asked again about what happened, he simply says, "I was blind but now I see" (John 9:25 NIV)!

I love his reply! He didn't try to quote Scripture or articulate theology. He didn't pull out a giant Post-it notepad and draw a diagram. He simply shared his story: "I was blind but now I see!" (That might make a good lyric for a song!)

Sharing Your Story

I think this once-blind man's story gives us a great framework for telling our own. It looks like this:

Part 1: My Life before Jesus

"I was blind," the man declared. That's who the man was before he met Jesus.

Part 2: How I Met Jesus

"He put mud on my eyes," the man would say. The man explains this strange first encounter with Jesus.

Accidental B.L.E.S.S.ing

 After going through training on the B.L.E.S.S. practices, a small group went out for coffee to debrief. They arrived at Starbucks, placed their orders, and sat down at a table where the conversation quickly turned to "How can we begin to do these practices as a group?" They discussed possible strategies to love their neighbors or the people with whom they worked. Then one member of the group said, "What about some other people we all walk past every day downtown—the homeless that struggle with shelter insecurity. Aren't they our neighbors? We see them every day by the train station." So the group agreed that was who they'd B.L.E.S.S.

The next Tuesday night, they gathered with a plan for building relationships with their nameless friends in need of shelter. They said a prayer and headed for the train station. With a couple of carafes of hot chocolate and plates of homemade cookies in hand, they walked up and down Ottawa Street, looking to be a blessing. There were no homeless people out. Someone suggested they look near the library two blocks away. They went, but there was no one. After about thirty minutes of searching, they realized that the people they'd see on the streets in the mornings were getting a free meal at a nearby refuge in the evenings.

Not to be stopped, the group was determined to give away their hot chocolate and cookies. So they went into the library and told the head librarian what they had hoped to do. To their surprise, she made an announcement that the library would soon be closing, and they were giving away free hot chocolate and cookies. Dozens of people stopped by on their way out and politely said "thanks" for the treats, then jumped into their cars and headed home. The group felt discouraged because they had spent their evening blessing those who were already blessed.

But one teenage girl who had been in the library stuck around after everyone else had left. Between bites of her second cookie, she told one of the women in the group that she had dropped out of school, feared she was addicted to cocaine, and didn't know where she would spend the night. After a few phone calls from the group to the right people, the young lady climbed into a minivan and headed to one of the group member's homes for the night.

Over the next few years, that girl experienced some ups and downs, but her overall trajectory was toward faith, Jesus, and a life of flourishing. With the group's help, she went through rehabilitation. She lived with one of the families in the group for eighteen months. She graduated from high school and said "yes" to becoming a Christ-follower. She was accepted to a Christian college, where she majored in social work.

During her first week there, she wrote a letter that was read to the small group members. "Thank you so much for having the faith three years ago to go downtown to simply bless people and ask, 'God, where are You at work?'" she wrote. "You have forever changed my life."

Part 3: My Life since I Met Jesus

"Oh, I was blind…BUT NOW I SEE!" That's how this man would explain the difference that Jesus made in his life!

Your Story

Each one of us has a story to share. And you'll want to have various versions of your story for different audiences and situations. Sometimes you'll have three minutes, other times maybe ten, or even as many as twenty or thirty minutes to share your story. Now I want to challenge you to share your story using the same framework.

Simple Tool for Storytelling

Three-Part Story

Let's use the once-blind man's story and a simple tool for learning how to tell our own story in three parts. I've used it to help me share my story with others and have taught numerous others to use it too. You wouldn't believe all the amazing stories that have come out of this simple framework. It looks like this:

Part 1: My Life before Jesus

What was your life like before you met Jesus? Or if you grew up in church knowing all about Jesus, what was your life like before you got serious about following Him? Your story begins with who you were.

_____

_____

_____

_____

_____

_____

_____

_____

Part 2: How I Met Jesus

How did you become a Christ-follower? Did you go through a particularly tough time in your life that led you to God? Did a friend invite you to a church service? Did a family member introduce you to Jesus? Did an experience inspire you to get serious about committing your life to Jesus?

_____

_____

_____

_____

_____

_____

_____

_____

_____

_____

_____

_____

_____

_____

Part 3: My Life since I Met Jesus

What difference has following Jesus made in your life? How has knowing Him impacted how you walk through both the good and the hard times in life? Yes, when you tell your story include both the good *and* hard times. People will be more impacted when you're honest about the challenges you continue to face even since choosing to follow Jesus. And don't give the easy Sunday School answer. Talk about how your life is different and how God is growing you in certain areas, but make sure you're sincere about how it's a process and how you still often get it wrong. Saint Francis Xavier said it well: "Speak to them the great mercy of God…. Sometimes people are helped by your telling of your own lamentable past."[2]

_____

_____

_____

_____

_____

_____

_____

_____

_____

_____

_____

_____

_____

Here are five tips to help you put your story on paper and memorize it.

ASK GOD FOR HELP. Before you write out and share your story, ask God for the words to say and insight about how to say it so that He can use it.

YOU BE YOU. Write out your three-part story the way you speak. Don't try to sound like someone else. It's your story and you just be you.

KEEP IT REAL. Don't sugarcoat or overdramatize your story. Tell the good, the bad, and the ugly just the way that it happened. Your authenticity will connect with others.

KEEP IT SHORT. Aim to keep your story three to five minutes long. At that length, it's easily something you can share in a conversation without turning it into a monologue or a sermon.

PRACTICE OUT LOUD. Once you have written your story out, practice it out loud several times until you feel like you are comfortable and could do it from memory.

Remember, you don't have to write a book. Just follow those five tips and compose a simple three- to five-minute version of your story in those three parts. Now you are ready to share it with your neighbor when they are ready.

Peter, Jesus's close friend and follower, challenged us in this way: "Always be prepared to give an answer to everyone who asks you to give the reason for the hope that you have" (1 Peter 3:15 NIV). Your answer is your story. Which brings us to the final challenge…

Ask God for an Opportunity to Share Your Story

There will be times when you'll need to use words, but remember it will be what people see in your life that gives your words credibility. So ask God for the chance to bless someone with your life and your story. Don't sanitize it or romanticize it. Simply tell your authentic story.

A friend of mine, Jen, used to be a self-described atheist. She felt that anyone who believed in Jesus would have to be simple-minded and uninformed. Today, she's a committed Christ-follower, but if you asked her how she came to know God, she wouldn't tell you about the intellectual and philosophical arguments for faith in Christ she heard along the way. She never had any trouble dismissing all of that in her mind.

What she would tell you is how a close friend shared her story of how Jesus radically changed her life. Jen said she didn't know what to do with that. It just kind of sat there inside her, tugging at her. She would say that her friend's story lived in her heart and mind for years. And when Jen wrestled with the idea of a God who loved her, it was her friend's story of what God had done in her life that made all the difference.

Nicodemus was forever changed after his late-night encounter when he heard Jesus's story. In that moment, he not only found forgiveness and a hope for eternity, but he also discovered his purpose. Later, John made sure to tell us that Nicodemus was one of two men who prepared the body of Jesus for burial after His crucifixion (John 19:39–42). Christian tradition and many biblical historians tell us that Nicodemus was so determined to bless the world in the name of Jesus that he was eventually martyred for refusing to deny his belief. He heard the story of Jesus and was changed forever.

Your story has that power too. Be bold, be willing to be stretched out of your comfort zone, and ask God for an opportunity to share it.

This second "S" in B.L.E.S.S. is the last of these five simple, every-day ways to B.L.E.S.S. your neighbor and change the world. In the next chapter, I want you to see how you can wake up every single morning ready to put these practices into action and bless others—yes, you heard me right. I said *every* day! Let me show you how.

B.L.E.S.S. DISCUSSION QUESTIONS

OPEN: What is your favorite story of all time? It could be a book, movie, or bedtime story from when you were a child.

_____

_____

_____

_____

DIG: Read John 3:1-17. What do you find most interesting about this encounter between Jesus and Nicodemus? How much of what Jesus said do you think Nicodemus understood?

_____

_____

_____

_____

_____

_____

When did you first come to understand the meaning of John 3:16? "For God so loved the world that he gave his one and only Son, that whoever believes in him shall not perish but have eternal life" (NIV). How would you convey the meaning and impact of these words if someone were to ask you about them?

_____

_____

_____

_____

Which of the "Reluctant Reasons" for sharing your story do you relate to most?

_____

_____

_____

Read John 9:1-11. How would you have felt if you were the man who was blind since birth and suddenly could see? How would you explain what happened?

_____

_____

_____

_____

What is your reaction to the simplicity of his story, "I was blind but now I see" (John 9:25)?

_____

_____

_____

_____

_____

REFLECT: If someone were to casually ask you, "How did you come to know the love of God in Jesus?" how would you respond?

_____

_____

_____

_____

CHAPTER 8

Are You Ready to Be a B.L.E.S.S.ing Every Day?

BIG IDEA
You can B.L.E.S.S. the people around you every day.

I think the whole world can be basically divided into three types of people: Nothing-to-Do people, Always-Something-to-Do people, and Have-to-Do people. I know which one I am. Which one are you? It's a lot more important than you might think. In fact, it is mission critical! Let me explain…

Nothing to Do

There are some people whose primary goal is to get everything done so they have "nothing to do." I'm not suggesting they actually have nothing to do; it's more about their motivation. They are motivated by the dream of someday having nothing to do. They live for the weekend, the next vacation, and eventually retirement. They live to rest. Their work is a means to only one end—that is, to arrive at a time and place where they have nothing they have to do.

Always-Something-to-Do

These people can't sit still; they find rest and Sabbath a struggle because they much prefer checking things off their "to-do" list as opposed to "sitting around." They are motivated by a goal and love of accomplishment. They live to get things done and are often seen as very successful. They live for the task. They often have a job, a "side hustle," run marathons, and maintain the best-looking lawn in the neighborhood. Their work is a series of tasks—and when the tasks are all completed, they create another to-do list.

Have-to-Do

These are the people who have a calling. By personality they may be a "Nothing-to-Do" person or an "Always-Something-to-Do" person, but a mission or grander vision has captured their imagination, and they discover a vocation they just "have to do." They are motivated by the truth that they are part of God's great work in the world and the knowledge that they are *created in Christ Jesus to do good works, which God prepared in advance for us to do*" (Ephesians 2:10). They live for that mission. Whether they have "nothing to do" or "always something to do," they wake up every morning knowing that God has something they "have to do."

My hope and prayer is that the B.L.E.S.S. way of living will move you from a "Nothing-to-Do" person OR an "Always-Something-to-Do" person to a "Have-to-Do" person. I'm convinced that if you wake up every morning and begin with prayer and look for ways to B.L.E.S.S. the people around you, you'll never again settle for a life filled with checking things off your "Always-Something-to-Do" list. You also won't be content with spending all your days sitting by the pool. While relaxation and accomplishment are good and needed, God has so much more for you. If you'll apply what you've learned from this book so far,

Slow is the new fast!

I had been using the B.L.E.S.S. practices for more than a year when I had two thoughts. First, "This really is a great way to build deep relationships with my neighbors." Secondly, "How long will it take before someone says 'yes' to Jesus?" I was in a hurry. I wanted results! And my preference was to see the results fast! However, B.L.E.S.S. just takes time. If you are like me and are tempted to hurry the process, you will end up driving people away instead of drawing them closer to you and God. They will feel like a project you are trying to complete rather than a person you love. So slow down and get it in your head now that God is responsible for converting; you are responsible for loving. With some people and in some contexts, you may move through all five practices quickly, and in others it may be months before you have a spiritual conversation. So just remind yourself that slow is the new fast!

I believe you will discover a mission for your life that is so compelling that you simply *have* to do it!

Why is this so important? Because Jesus was a "Have-to-Do" person, and it is "Have-to-Do" people who change the world!

Jesus's Have-to-Do Moment

John tells us about a time when Jesus felt, I simply *"have to do this."* The beginning of this story often goes unnoticed, but it starts like this: *"Jesus left Judea and set out once more for Galilee. But he had to pass through Samaria"* (John 4:3–4 NET).

I think if we read between the lines, we can see that Jesus thought to Himself, *I have to go through Samaria because there is someone there that I simply have to meet and bless!*

A little homework indicates that there was actually something behind His decision because Jewish people avoided Samaria at all costs. The Samaritans and the Jews hated each other. They were enemies.

In Samaria, Jesus met a woman at a well where the whole community went for water. But this woman was there at an odd time. She came when no one else was there, especially the women of the village. The truth is that she had been married five times, and Guy Number Six, whom she was currently living with, wasn't her husband. She was all alone because she was a woman with personal failures and a questionable reputation. The community had rejected her, and that was likely why she went to the well all by herself when she did.

But the stigma of her being a Samaritan and a woman with a questionable reputation didn't stop Jesus from approaching her. It was for her that Jesus said, "I have to go where no one else wants to go." He was on a mission. He was intent on blessing her.

Jesus not only engaged her in conversation, but He also treated her with dignity; He loved her, and He blessed her! As a result, Jesus changed her life. She went from being someone who went to the well at the hottest time of day to avoid being noticed to becoming a woman so compelled by the love of Jesus that she went back into the village to tell everyone about her life-changing experience. John notes that she left her water jar, went back into town, and told her neighbors, "Come, see a man who told me everything that I did. Can this be the Christ" (John 4:29 NLT)?

This story offers us three very important discoveries we should apply as Christ-followers: First, we discover that Jesus had a mission. He had a cause that was so compelling He woke up every day thinking, *This is what I have to do!*

Beware of B.L.E.S.S. moralism.

All spiritual disciplines have the potential for great good as well as great harm. When we integrate these disciplines into the rhythm of our everyday life with the full knowledge that God relentlessly loves us, they can help us grow closer to Him and to others. However, when we start to measure our own worth based on whether we have prayed, fasted, or done one of the B.L.E.S.S. practices, we can easily slip into moralism. We need to always be on the alert for allowing a list of spiritual activities to determine our value; instead, we want our value to always be decided by a good and gracious God. So if you find you are patting yourself on the back when do you these practices or beating yourself up when you don't, you may have slipped into moralism. Remember this: God loves you just as you are and not as you should be. Let that determine your worth—and with that knowledge, live out the B.L.E.S.S. practices.

Second, as followers of Jesus, we too have a mission! We have a compelling cause and a calling that there is something we have to do every single day!

And finally, if we're attuned to the Spirit of Jesus at work in our lives and bring some prayerful effort to this, we will be on mission every day. We will B.L.E.S.S. the people around us just like Jesus blessed the people around Him.

B.L.E.S.S.ing on the El

Lauren Seaman is a "Have-to-Do" person. He has a calling that transforms an average workday into an adventure with God. He also understands that loving your neighbor one person at a time is what changes the world. Here is just one of his many stories in his own words...

While living in Chicago the B.L.E.S.S. practices were part of my everyday life. It was something I loved doing and felt a calling to do. I was always praying for people I came across, looking and listening for opportunities to share the love of Jesus through the course of my day.

One day I was on the "el" (that's the elevated train in Chicago) heading into the city. It was about two in the afternoon and there was a guy sitting next to me. I noticed that he was copying English sentences from one piece of paper to another, so I inferred that he was learning English.

What you need to know about me is that I grew up in Côte d'Ivoire in West Africa, so I recognized him as being West African. I said, "Hey, do you mind if I ask...are you learning English? He said, "Yes." And I said, "Do you mind if I ask where you are from?" And he said, "Oh, a small country in West Africa. You wouldn't know of it." I said, "Give it a try." And he said, "Ivory Coast," which is the English translation of Côte d'Ivoire. I said, "Are you kidding me? Only God could put two Ivory Coast brothers on a train together on a Wednesday afternoon in a city of three million people." Immediately, his eyes lit up, he stood up, and he embraced me.

His name was Ibrahim, and over the course of the next few months we became great friends. I would like to tell you that I shared the Gospel with him that day, and that when we got off the train, we walked to the lakefront where I baptized him right then and there. That's not what happened, but what God did through that relationship as I lived out these B.L.E.S.S. practices was nothing short of miraculous.

Because of my friendship with Ibrahim, we were able to get involved in the immigration process for several spouses of his friends to help them get to the U.S. legally. We served these families in numerous ways as they adjusted to their new life in the U.S. Being new to the country and not having a good grasp of the English language meant that Ibrahim and most of his male friends were working as dishwashers in local restaurants, barely making enough money to survive. Over time, I was able to refer them to a contractor who hired them as welders, doubling their income.

We had something we called Table Life, where every Wednesday we would invite people to share a meal with us in our home. Ibrahim brought numerous friends to join us for Table Life. We all know Chicago is one of the most divided cities in our country, but Table Life became a safe space where a Muslim refugee from the north side, a Hispanic immigrant from the south side, an African American kid from the west side, a widow from across the street, and a neighbor next door could all get to know and understand each other over a meal in a way that only God could orchestrate.

As we got to know each other better, Ibrahim invited me to several Ramadan feasts. And on more than one occasion, during those feasts, the conversation would turn to Jesus, who He was, and what Christianity was all about. At times I felt like I was having an out-of-body experience. And I know for many Christians that would be a very threatening environment, but because of the power of the Holy Spirit, lots of prayer, sharing meals together, and serving one another, we were able to have this kind of open and life-giving dialogue.

B.L.E.S.S.ing the firm

A church in New Jersey developed a curriculum for members to be trained in the B.L.E.S.S. practices. Rosa, a senior-level manager at a national consulting firm in New York, was one of the first people to go through it. Since she had earned a great deal of respect at work, she chose to make that the focus of her efforts.

Rosa began praying for her coworkers by name. From time to time, she would go to work early in the morning and do a sort of prayer walk through the offices of her building, praying for each coworker as she passed by their office or cubicle. She focused on being a better listener and asking more open-ended questions during one-on-one meetings, like "What do you like to do when you're not working?" or "Tell me more about your family." She was also more intentional about lunch breaks, asking God to give her opportunities to share meals with staffers who might need some encouragement or direction.

One day one of the people she had been praying for and sharing lunches with started pinging Rosa with odd messages through the office's internal communication system. It was as if she wanted to talk about something, but she wasn't being clear. Finally, she wrote, "Rosa, I think I need to talk to you." Rosa quickly responded, "I'm here whenever you need me. Just let me know when you can come by my office." A few hours later, there was a knock on Rosa's office door. That led to a series of conversations and eventually a growing friendship between Rosa and her coworker, and they began to study the Bible together.

Rosa continued to serve her employees in such remarkable ways that senior executives took notice. Not only was her team working better together, but production was also improving. Her supervisors saw a significant transformation—one they wanted to see replicated with other teams.

The firm held regular town hall meetings. Rosa was asked to share the secrets behind her leadership style—why she led the way she led and how others could apply similar practices. Her presentation was so well-received that she was asked to share it with the highest leaders in the organization. And at the end, Rosa said, "By the way, all of these principles are found in the life and person of Jesus."

I will never forget what Ibrahim told me one time after we had been friends for several years. He said, "I don't fully understand everything about Jesus, but I want to spend the rest of my life learning more about Him." We then started reading the Bible together.

I can't help but wonder how many of us travel up and down the el every day and completely miss Kingdom opportunities, Gospel opportunities, all around us. There are no limits to how God can use these B.L.E.S.S. practices. It takes intentionality and purpose. But I am convinced that if we are motivated by the great commandment—to love God and to love our neighbors—God will work through us to love our neighbors and change the world.

Become a "Have-to-Do" Person

"*How did the two of us end up together?*" That is not the kind of question you want to hear from your wife. I would much prefer to be asked, "How come you are so good-looking?" (I'm still waiting on that question) or "How come you are so smart?" (more waiting!) In this case, Sue was asking it rhetorically after proofing the first few paragraphs of this chapter about the world being divided into three types of people. Sue and I have very different personalities. Sue is more of a "Nothing-to-Do" person and I'm more of an

"Always-Something-to-Do" person. Let me clarify. (I don't want something in print that will get me in trouble!) Sue works very hard. She is a gifted leader in her job, and she goes above and beyond as a mom and wife. But what she looks forward to and enjoys is having fun and doing nothing. She plans the vacations. She makes sure we have a Sabbath. Sue is more of a "Nothing-to-Do" person. Me? I always have something to do. I love a checklist, and I get an adrenaline rush checking each box. Just look at my bio on the author page and it will tell you that I'm too driven and slightly too dependent on the rush of accomplishment.

However, it's when we both use the B.L.E.S.S. practices to love our neighbors that God transforms both of us from "Nothing-to-Do" and "Always-Something-to-Do" people into "Have-to-Do" people. The rhythm of B.L.E.S.S. living takes the focus off of us and what we want and puts the focus on others and what God wants! When we do that, we begin to "love the Lord our God with all our heart and all our soul and with all our mind and with all our strength (and) 'love our neighbor as ourself'" (Mark 12:30–31). It changes us…and our world…and it changes both us and the world for the better!

I want you to join me on this mission to change the world by loving our neighbors. I want to ask you to commit to making the B.L.E.S.S. practices something you "have to do."

Will you do that? Will you join me?

I believe you want to love your neighbors and change the world. I believe you want to be on mission. You might even say you *have* to be on mission. My question to you is this: Are you willing to adopt a new way of living, a new system or set of behaviors that will help you bless the people around you so that more of them will come to know the love of God in Jesus?

If you are ready to commit to being a blessing to others, I want to ask you to respond in two ways: first, by signing the B.L.E.S.S. Pledge (see next page); and second, by sharing it with two friends, neighbors, or family members who will also sign it.

I'm serious about this being more than a moment when you nod your head in agreement and keep on reading. I am asking you to sign your name, put a date on it, and have two witnesses—people you see frequently—sign it as well. I want this to be a genuine pledge between you, God, and two other people who will hold you accountable.

Congratulations on almost finishing this book! Please don't stop here. Because in the last chapter I'm going to give you a step-by-step plan for how you and your friends can take the B.L.E.S.S. rhythms and multiply them in others. I'll reveal how the blessing strategy God gave us in Genesis was designed to change the whole world! Yes, all of it! It's going to make so much sense. Trust me.

B.L.E.S.S. Discussion Questions

OPEN: Are you more of a "Nothing-to-Do" or an "Always-Something-to-Do" or a "Have-to-Do" person? Why?

_____

_____

_____

_____

_____

_____

_____

B.L.E.S.S. PLEDGE

Jesus commanded us to be a blessing to the world around us when He said, "Love your neighbor as yourself" (Mark 12:31). In obedience to that command, I pledge to do one of the following five B.L.E.S.S practices every day:

B: BEGIN WITH PRAYER

I pledge to pray for my neighbors. My example is Jesus, who started His earthly mission with prayer (Luke 6:12–16). Prayer is both how I discover my mission and how I do the mission of Jesus.

L: LISTEN

I pledge to listen to my neighbors. My example is Jesus, who loved others by asking questions and then listening to them (Luke 18:40–42). Listening is how I give dignity to others, and it is a gracious expression of love.

E: EAT

I pledge to eat with my neighbors. My example is Jesus, who consistently shared meals with the "sinners" (Matthew 9:9–13). Eating with others is how I move a relationship from an acquaintance to a friendship.

S: SERVE

I pledge to serve my neighbors. My example is Jesus, who did not come to be served, but to serve others (Matthew 20:28). Serving others is a tangible way I can demonstrate the love of God to others.

S: STORY

I pledge to share my story with my neighbors. My example is Jesus, who shared the good news of His own story with others (John 3:1–17). Sharing my story gives others a clear understanding of how God's love and the life of Jesus can change their lives.

_____

Signed (your name, today's date)

_____   _____
Witness #1 (name and date)   Witness #2 (name and date)

For a printer-friendly version of this pledge, please visit bless-book.org.

DIG: Read John 4:1–42. What strikes you as most interesting about this encounter between Jesus and the Samaritan woman? What are some of the ways that Jesus blessed her?

_____

_____

_____

_____

_____

If someone were to ask you, "What does it mean to love your neighbor?" how would you respond?

_____

_____

_____

_____

Which of these everyday ways to love your neighbor and change the world do you most look forward to practicing? Which one will you find most challenging? Explain.

_____

_____

_____

_____

What would it take for you to become a "Have-to-Do" person with regard to "loving your neighbors?"

_____

_____

_____

_____

_____

REFLECT: Who are the eight people you want to B.L.E.S.S.?

_____

_____

_____

_____

Are you willing to sign the B.L.E.S.S. Pledge and commit to blessing the people around you every day?

_____

_____

_____

_____

_____

_____

CHAPTER 9

A B.L.E.S.S. Strategy for Changing the World

BIG IDEA
When we B.L.E.S.S. together, we can change the world.

"**C**an I start something for my friends who won't come to church?"
I was surprised to hear Kathy, a social worker, say this because she uses the B.L.E.S.S. practices every day, and on Sundays she routinely brings people to church who are far from God. I might even look out into the crowd at a service and see an entire row of Kathy's friends sitting next to her. Kathy is as passionate about loving her neighbors and changing the world as I am. Probably more!

So when Kathy told me about the young women in the eating-disorder group she was leading and said, "I'm not sure I can get them to come to church with me," I had to listen. She went on to tell me that the girls were intimidated to go into the auditorium with several hundred other people present. They had actually tried before—but even though some of them ventured into the building, they stayed in the lobby the whole time.

That led to Kathy's question: "Can I start something for my friends who won't come to church?"

The question challenged my thinking in several ways, but I knew the answer had to be "Yes!"

149

God Is Always Going and Sending

Kathy's spiritual instincts were right on: rather than wait for others to come to her, she wanted to go to them. Her heart was aligned with God's.

God has been clear about His desire for us to love our neighbors by initiating relationships. We started with this idea back in the introduction. But what might be new to you is that God has always loved people (including you and me) by initiating a relationship. All throughout the Bible, He takes the lead and asks those who love Him to do the same.

God loved and blessed Abram, but then God sent Abram to go to a foreign land to be a blessing: "Leave your country, your people and your father's household and go to the land I will show you. I will make you into a great nation and I will bless you...and you will be a blessing to others" (Genesis 12 NIV).

God loved His Son, but then He sent Jesus to us and initiated a relationship with us when He "became flesh and blood, and moved into the neighborhood" (John 1:14 MSG).

Jesus initiated a loving relationship with His first followers and disciples and asked them to do the same: "The Lord appointed seventy-two others and sent them two by two ahead of him to every town and place he was about to go. He told them 'The harvest is plentiful, but the workers are few. Ask the Lord of the harvest, therefore to send out workers into his harvest field. Go! I am sending you...'" (Luke 10).

Over and over, our God initiates, and God's people go! In fact, those are Jesus's parting word to His disciples: "Go and make disciples of all nations..." (Matthew 28). From the beginning of the Bible to the end, we are reminded that the mission of God is to "go" and love people where they live, work, and play.

Isn't there something inside you that knows you have to get beyond the walls of your home? Isn't it unrealistic to insist that the rest of the

You need accountability to B.L.E.S.S.

Experts say it takes twenty-one days to establish a habit, but in my experience, it only takes thirty days to forget about that habit. This applies to the B.L.E.S.S. practices as well. In order to maintain this missional habit and turn it into a lifestyle, you will need accountability, such as a group that starts and begins its weekly meeting with the question: "Who did you B.L.E.S.S. this week?" Or you will need the accountability of a church that shares inspiring stories of using the B.L.E.S.S. practices and then challenges you to share a story about the people you have had a chance to B.L.E.S.S. Make the B.L.E.S.S. practices a habit by doing them for twenty-one straight days. Make it a lifestyle by being accountable to others who remind you of your commitment to this habit at least once a month.

world must come to us so we can love them? We certainly can't passively wait for our neighbors to wander inside our church buildings before we love them! That's what Kathy believed when she asked me, "Can I start something for my friends who won't come to church?" Once we gave her permission, she formed a small group of young women and began to multiply the blessing.

Before I tell you how she did that, let me back up and tell you how she was blessed.

"Treat Them Like They're Christians Till They Realize They're Not"

"I don't think I've ever seen anyone become a Christian," Matt told me. He was my new small-group apprentice leader. Matt had grown up going to church every Sunday and was as thoroughly "churched" as anyone I'd ever met! As a kid, he was in church on Sunday morning, Sunday night, and Wednesday night. As a student, his best friends were in the church youth group. When he left home and went to college, he quickly joined a campus ministry that became his new social circle and filled his calendar with Christian activities. For his whole life, Christians had surrounded Matt.

But things were about to change for Matt. He was now a part of a small group I led where the vision was to love our neighbors and the strategy was to use the B.L.E.S.S. practices. I had seen the power of a small group committed to blessing others. People who are searching spiritually are looking for friends with whom they can talk (see Chapter 1). My experience was that once you're friends with someone, it's not weird, awkward, or unusual for you to invite them to meet some of your other friends. And that is what a small group is—simply a group of friends.

I had invited a couple new friends to join our group who were searching spiritually. One of them was Kathy; the other was her Oxford-educated husband with a Ph.D., Richard. Just before my friends arrived, I told Matt, "You just watch; if they stick around in this group, they'll say 'yes' to following Jesus."

They did stick around. My two new friends became friends with the others in that small group. Kathy and Richard asked lots of questions. We also shared a lot of laughs, honest conversations, many meals, and some great times. We have a slogan in our small groups: "Treat them like they're Christians till they realize they're not." After several months of becoming friends with my friends, Kathy and Richard realized they were not followers of Jesus and decided that needed to change.

It was so fun to be there with Matt when they were baptized. I couldn't resist pulling Matt aside and whispering, "See, I told you, if they just would just stick around, they'd say 'yes' to Jesus."

Don't lose your sense of urgency.

There is a grace that comes to anyone who uses the B.L.E.S.S. practices. That grace takes the pressure off you to "save" somebody because we recognize that only God can save. The practices are also a relational process that slowly guides us in doing our part to simply love our neighbors and, over time, introduce them to the love of God. That is right and so good. At the same time, there is a real urgency in sharing the good news of Jesus with our neighbors and friends. 2 Corinthians 6:2 says "now is the day of salvation." 1 Peter 3:9 reminds us that God doesn't want "anyone to perish but everyone to come to repentance." Relax in the grace of knowing that God alone can save but seek where God is working with an urgency that eternities depend on.

Multiplying the B.L.E.S.S.ing

Having been a recipient of the blessing, Kathy was now using the B.L.E.S.S. practices with the young women in the eating-disorder small group that she led on Tuesday nights. As God used her to bless one young woman after another, the group began to change. Instead of this recovery group existing only for the members of the group, it began to exist for others outside the group. As the women in the group began to find God and healing, they began to look for others who needed God and healing in their lives.

I distinctly remember a Saturday night when Kathy had the privilege of baptizing Kristin, a young woman from her group. Her journey to that moment was both painful and miraculous.

Kathy had prayed for Kristin, listened to her, shared meals with her, and served her by helping in her recovery. Despite the friendship and love that Kathy showered on Kristin, she continued to spiral downward. The diseases of anorexia and bulimia were slowly taking away the life of this beautiful twenty-one-year-old. The doctors told Kristin that her vital organs were threatening to shut down and that she had permanently damaged her liver. It was then that Kristin asked Kathy if she would pray for her and ask God to do a miracle.

Kathy prayed.

And God did a miracle!

According to the doctors, her liver improved. Medically, it was impossible, but it couldn't be denied. The doctors couldn't explain it. Kristin couldn't explain it! But Kathy offered an explanation: "It's God answering our prayer." It was an eye-opening experience for Kristin, and she decided to give her life to the Jesus that Kathy told her about. Several weeks later on a Saturday night, Kathy was able to baptize Kristin. All the girls from the recovery group were there to support Kristin as she acknowledged her ultimate higher power.

Afterward, the group went out to celebrate together. At the encouragement of the other girls, Kristin took the opportunity to share her story. As she told about the healing miracle God had done in her body and spirit, one of the other girls in the group, Tara, spoke up and said, "I need that...that is exactly what I need." So one day after Kathy baptized Kristin, Kristin baptized Tara!

I told you that using the B.L.E.S.S. practices is an adventure!

Four Generations of B.L.E.S.S.ing

This is exactly what God envisioned when He gave us the B.L.E.S.S. strategy. The blessing is supposed to be multiplied from person to person to person.

Jesus had a vision that the blessing would be multiplied from "Jerusalem, and in all Judea and Samaria, and to the ends of the earth" (Acts 1:8).

The Apostle Paul shared that vision of multiplying the blessing with his young apprentice, Timothy, when he said, "And the things you have heard me say in the presence of many witnesses entrust to reliable people who will also be qualified to teach others" (2 Timothy 2:2 NIV). In the same way that Paul challenged Timothy with four generations of blessing multiplication, I got to see it happen from me to Tara.

Paul —> Timothy —> many witnesses —> reliable people
Dave —> Kathy —> Kristin —> Tara

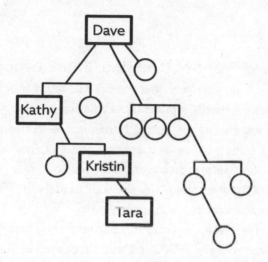

So how do you multiply a B.L.E.S.S. group? Keep it simple! You and your apprentice will lead this group, and you two will want to meet (either face to face or online) at least weekly outside of the group. When you think your apprentice is ready to lead a B.L.E.S.S. group and your apprentice also thinks he or she is ready to lead, it's time to multiply! Send them out to be blessings! If you want to learn more about multiplying apprentice leaders, I encourage you to read my book *Hero Maker: Five Essential Practices for Leaders to Multiply Leaders* (Zondervan, 2018).[1] It will give you all you need to know.

This world-changing strategy that God gave us was designed so that "all peoples on earth will be blessed by you" (Genesis 12:3 NIV). By who? Reread the verse. By you! The ability to multiply the blessing is something you can do—and it's almost as simple as the ability to be a blessing.

It only requires you and a small group of friends or neighbors who will make two commitments! Let me explain the two types of B.L.E.S.S. small groups and then the two commitments you all need to make...

Two Types of B.L.E.S.S. Small Groups

The Bible is crystal clear that we are far better together than we are alone. Jesus's words remind us of this truth: "For where two or more come together in my name, I am there with them" (Matthew 18:20 NLT). Jesus is telling us that He is present in a qualitatively different way when we're together, rather than alone.

And Jesus's prayer in John 17 was "that all of them may be one...so that they may be brought to complete unity." Why did Jesus want us to come together? Why was unity so important? "Then the world will know that you sent me and have loved them even as you have loved me" (John 21:21, 23). Jesus is saying that when we unify, collaborate, and come together to bless the world, He will be more present AND people will experience the love of God.

Creating a small group to bless the world can start with just two people—you and a friend! It can also start with more than two—like twelve! That is what Jesus did! The number isn't as important as the act of linking arms with others who share your passion to love their neighbors and change their world through the B.L.E.S.S.ing strategy. Find people like you who know this is something they "have to do."

This B.L.E.S.S. small group should get clear on how the members are going to practice the rhythms of blessing others. Let me give you two basic ways you can do it:

B.L.E.S.S. Group (Common Mission)

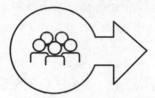

The first type of B.L.E.S.S. group is one with a common mission. A common mission is when all the people in the group share the same mission. A good example is the story I told about Kathy and how her eating-disorder recovery group all adopted the mission of helping other women with eating disorders find healing with the help of God. What makes a B.L.E.S.S. group with a common mission unique is that all members of the group share the exact same mission. The shared mission could be to bless a particular group of people or to bless a particular neighborhood or community.

B.L.E.S.S. Group (Multiple Missions)

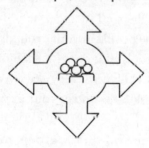

The second type of B.L.E.S.S. group is one with multiple missions—a variety of different people they are seeking to bless.

This group could consist of one person who wants to bless her neighborhood and another person who wants to bless the Little League team he coaches. Another may want to bless the office where she works while someone else may want to bless a group of guys who are gaming every Friday night. They all want to be blessings, and they come together to hold each other accountable for blessing the people God has put in their lives.

Two Commitments of a B.L.E.S.S. Small Group

Now that you understand the two types of B.L.E.S.S. small groups, let me make sure you understand the two commitments that everyone in the group should make.

Commitment #1: Use One B.L.E.S.S. Practice Every Day

This first commitment is obvious, but so essential. You cannot be a blessing if you're not blessing others. The only reason the B.L.E.S.S. strategy hasn't worked the way God intended is because we haven't used it on a consistent basis like He intended!

To ensure that your small group understands the five everyday ways to be a blessing, make sure all the members have a copy of this book. Go through the book together and use the B.L.E.S.S. discussion questions to help them all to understand how to live out each of the practices. Assist the people in your group by helping them understand the five simple tools that go with each of the practices so they can easily live out B.L.E.S.S. every day. And definitely use the B.L.E.S.S. Pledge to ask everyone in your group to commit to using the practices.

If you are leading the B.L.E.S.S. group, make sure you're doing one of these practices every day! Leaders reproduce who they are. The speed of the leader = the speed of the team. If you do it, the group will follow. One of the ways I ensure I do at least one practice every day is to always begin my day with prayer. I write out the word B.L.E.S.S. in my journal, then I do what I've asked you to do throughout this book: I write down the names of eight of my neighbors.

At the core of creating a small group that will be a blessing is people who are using the B.L.E.S.S. practices every day. Without that you will not be a blessing. It's that simple!

Commitment #2: Begin Your Group by Asking, "Who Did You B.L.E.S.S.?"

Accountability is like a good coach: it helps you do something you might never do on your own. Your group needs to provide accountability by always asking at the start of each group, "Who did you B.L.E.S.S.?" Knowing this question is coming will help keep everyone focused on the people you want to bless.

Sometimes people ask me, "Does it count if I just pray?" Yes, that counts! It's actually how the blessing begins—God working in you to work in others! So whether it's praying, listening, eating, serving, or telling your story—make sure you're doing one practice each day and check in on each other by asking, "Who did you B.L.E.S.S.?"

If you create a B.L.E.S.S. small group around those two commitments, God will bless it, He'll bless you, and you will bless your neighbor and maybe the world. That's what happened with Shawn ...

"I Think I Accidentally Planted a Church"

I end with Shawn's story because he's an everyday Christ-follower like you and me who used the B.L.E.S.S. practices. Although Shawn's story does have a surprising ending.

Shawn liked church, but he was growing frustrated because his closest friends had no interest in it. He often would ask them to join him, but the answer was typically and often "no."

But Shawn knew that if he asked his friends to go water skiing, the answer was always "yes." They would rearrange their schedules and do whatever it took to be out on the water with him.

This gave Shawn an idea. He changed his Sunday routine from going to church to going out for breakfast and then water skiing with a couple of his best buds for whom he routinely prayed.

On the first Sunday he played hooky from church to go skiing with his two non-Christian friends, he was about to get in the boat when he got an attack of the "guilties." So he said, "Guys, you know I'm Baptist, and I'm feeling kind of guilty for not being in church today. Do you mind if I read a bit of Scripture first?" It was Shawn's boat, so his friends shrugged, "OK." Shawn read the shortest Psalm he could find.

Then Shawn added, "We Baptists also pray for needs, so do either of you have any prayer requests?" There was moment of awkward silence. Finally, one of the guys reminded them he was unemployed, and then the other chimed in, saying his grandma was in the ICU. So Shawn prayed for his friend's job search and the other guy's grandmother, and then he asked God to bless their day on the boat. Then they went skiing.

The next Sunday, at Shawn's encouragement, his two friends brought several of their own friends to also go water skiing. Once again Shawn didn't feel right about missing church, so before they left, he asked if he could read a little Scripture. Everyone nodded, "OK." He read a verse and got ready to pray. But this time he said, "We Baptists like to see if there are any answered prayers." To Shawn's surprise, the first friend said, "You know, I did get a job this week, thanks!" Then the other friend let everyone know, "My grandma was released from the hospital this week!" Then Shawn asked if there were any other prayer requests. After hearing those kinds of results, a bunch of hands went up. Shawn prayed for each one of them, asked God to bless the day, and then went skiing.

Shawn and his friends now do this weekly with more than sixty people. They gather near the dock, have breakfast, read a bit of Scripture, pray for each other, and then go water skiing. After they had been doing this for several weeks, one of the guys suggested they collect spare boat parts so they could help others out if somebody's boat broke down. So they began to make that part of their weekly gathering as well.

Shawn looks back on this and says, "I think I accidentally planted a church."

That's what a B.L.E.S.S. small group can look like.

That's how you love your neighbor.

And that is how we can change your world!

Change Your World!

We started with my confessing how I made sharing the good news feel really bad—for both my neighbors and me! Thanks to God's Word, the life of Jesus, and some solid research, we now know ...

That the good news was not meant to be shared through relationally awkward conversations with strangers, but in routine exchanges between friends and neighbors.

That the Christian life is not to be lived so silently that your friends would have no clue as to why you live the way you live; it's a story that you live first and then share.

That the Gospel is not composed of memorized formulas or trick questions you use on strangers, but is something that fits easily into your everyday life.

God promised, "all peoples on earth will be blessed through you" (Genesis 12:3 NIV).

You now know the five everyday ways to bless your neighbor.

Go change your world!

B.L.E.S.S. DISCUSSION QUESTIONS

OPEN: What is your fondest memory of being on a team or with a group of people who accomplished something greater than they could have on their own?

_____

_____

_____

_____

_____

_____

DIG: Read Genesis 12:1–3 and Luke 10:1–3. What do these passages tell you about the character and nature of God?

_____

_____

_____

_____

_____

_____

_____

_____

One of Jesus's last statements to His closest followers was, "Go and make disciples of all nations." To "go" may mean going somewhere in particular, like a move across town or across the globe. It also means "as you go" wherever you go, to be a blessing. Where do you believe God is asking you to go to be a B.L.E.S.S.ing?

_____

_____

_____

_____

_____

Why do we resist God's call to go? What excuses do we let stand in the way of following this command?

_____

_____

_____

_____

What is your reaction to the story of how Shawn started a church on the dock with his water-skiing friends?

_____

_____

_____

_____

_____

Matthew 18:20 reminds us: "For where two or more come to-gether in my name, I am there with them" (NET). How does this verse encourage you to be on mission with others to B.L.E.S.S. the people around you? Can you think of someone or a group of people with whom you could start a B.L.E.S.S. small group?

_____

_____

_____

_____

REFLECT: What do you need to do in order to follow through on these two commitments?

Commitment #1: Use one B.L.E.S.S. practice every day.

Commitment #2: Begin your group by asking, "Who did you B.L.E.S.S.?"

_____

_____

_____

_____

_____

_____

B.L.E.S.S. during a Pandemic

As I write these words, we are now many months into what we know as the COVID-19 pandemic. I have no idea how history will record this season, but I chose to include this in the book because it provides a great example of how these B.L.E.S.S. practices can be put into action under almost any circumstances.

In the initial phase of the crisis, most people's attention was focused on adjusting to what many called a "new normal." For many across the globe, this meant abiding by stay-at-home orders issued by local and state governments. For pastors and church leaders in particular, it meant shifting to digital church and putting all sorts of leadership energy into online services and small groups using Zoom and similar technology. People were isolated, desperately needing connection and to know they weren't alone.

While our church staff was making the shift to online services and groups, we quickly realized that while we were under a "stay-at-home" order there would be more opportunities than ever to bless our neighbors. We repeated this mantra: "Where fear sees a crisis, faith sees an opportunity"—convinced that this crisis would give us the opportunity to live out our mission in unprecedented ways.

One way we did this was by working with local nonprofits to identify the top ten to twelve emerging needs in our communities. We then developed teams to address them—loneliness teams, food insecurity teams, teams to serve high-risk individuals, and many more. Through these teams we were able to mobilize hundreds of people to bless thousands of people across Chicagoland.

We also knew that staying at home did not mean we would stop blessing the neighbors all around us. So when Jon met with a group of leaders at Community via Zoom, he shared with them what it could look like for each of us as individuals to remain on mission and share the love of Jesus by being a blessing to our neighbors, even under a "stay-at-home" order.

Here are the notes from that gathering:

B: BEGIN WITH PRAYER. You can continue to pray for your neighbors. If you need some help, go to BlessEveryHome.com. It lists your neighbors' names and addresses with helpful ideas for how you can pray for them. You could go on a prayer walk through your neighborhood as long you wear a mask and maintain social-distancing guidelines. Ask God to bless the people you see or the apartment buildings, homes, and businesses in your neighborhood as you walk through your community.

L: LISTEN. As long as you keep your distance (six feet apart at that time), you can still talk to people when you are out and about. If you aren't comfortable leaving your home or if you are a high-risk individual, then use FaceTime, Zoom, or Google Hangout with friends, neighbors, and coworkers. Ask them, "How are you doing?" and then give them the space to actually tell you how they are doing. More than ever in this season of isolation, people are longing for connection—someone who will LISTEN to them.

E: EAT. Offer to provide a meal via a food-delivery app. Or better yet, don't ask first. Surprise someone. Buy a delicious "treat" at the grocery store and drop it off for someone. Schedule a Zoom lunch or dinner together. Just this week a couple of our leaders delivered some freshly baked scones to their neighbors. My wife, Lisa, and I were on the receiving end of a blessing when someone from her small group left a loaf of Easter bread on our front porch.

S: SERVE. Social-distancing means we have to get creative in how we serve others: Write a thank-you note to your local grocer or first responders, etc. Share toilet paper (it is a very hot commodity) or other supplies with your neighbors. Call someone who may be lonely or buy groceries for someone who can't leave their home.

S: STORY. In this crisis we may have more opportunities than ever to tell our story of how we found our way to God and the difference our hope in Jesus makes, especially during these difficult times. Look for opportunities to share your story. And keep it simple. It's as easy as one, two, three: 1) your life before you met Jesus, 2) how you met Jesus, and 3) your life since you met Jesus.

I share this with you because it is a tremendous reminder that we can bless our neighbors under any and all circumstances. The mission of Jesus is simply unstoppable when every Christ-follower recognizes the opportunities around them and the responsibility before them to help people experience the love of Jesus.

B.L.E.S.S. Resources

www.BLESS-Book.org: The official website for *B.L.E.S.S.: 5 Everyday Ways to Love Your Neighbor and Change the World.* Here you can find resources created by the authors and many other leaders, churches, networks, and denominations that use the B.L.E.S.S. practices. This website is constantly being updated with tools that will help you use the B.L.E.S.S. practices more effectively.

www.daveferguson.org: The website for Dave Ferguson, listing all his books, resources, and how to contact him.

www.jonferguson.org: The website for Jon Ferguson, listing all his books, resources, and how to contact him.

www.communitychristian.org: The website for Community Christian Church, a multisite missional community that helps people find their way back to God.

www.CommunityOnline.tv: The website for celebration services of Community Christian Church.

www.newthing.org: The website for NewThing, a global church-planting movement with a mission to catalyze more movements of reproducing churches.

www.Exponential.org: The website for Exponential, which provides thoughtful leadership to equip movement-makers to accelerate the multiplication of healthy, reproducing faith communities.

List of B.L.E.S.S. Basics

List of B.L.E.S.S. Stories

When you write a book with the title *B.L.E.S.S.*, it only makes sense that you acknowledge some people who have blessed you. These are the people who prayed for us, listened to us, have eaten with us, served us, and shared their stories with us. You have been a blessing in our lives.

Acknowledgments from Dave:

First, I want to thank my wife, Sue. She is far better at using the B.L.E.S.S. practices with others than I am. Thank you for being the greatest single blessing in my life. Thank you for being both a co-creator and editor of my work and offering invaluable feedback. Thank you, and I love you!

Thank you to Amy, Josh, and Caleb. While I have tried to be a blessing in your lives, what you have given back to me is a blessing one thousand times greater. I love you, and I am cheering you on as you pass along the blessings to others through your life and your work.

Thank you to my brother, Jon Ferguson, who has partnered with me on almost every venture in my life, from D & J Lawn Care as kids to co-founding Community Christian Church and NewThing! Jon, being your brother and your partner in the world's greatest cause has been an extraordinary blessing.

Acknowledgments from Jon:

To start, I want to thank my wife, Lisa. You are the most resilient and loyal person I know. Time and time again you have seen in me what I have often not seen in myself. Your constant encouragement, loving support, and steady example of what it means to B.L.E.S.S. our neighbors are an endless source of inspiration to me. I truly love you!

Thank you, Graham and Chloe, for the honor and blessing of being your dad. I am so proud of how you B.L.E.S.S. the people around you in some of the most exhilarating and yet challenging places in the world. You give me hope that the trajectory of the Jesus mission is strong as I watch you genuinely love people the way Jesus loves people.

To my brother, Dave. Some of life's greatest blessings are the ones that have always been. And to me, you have always been…from sharing a trundle bed when we were kids to rooming together in college to leading these amazing missions that we call Community and NewThing. Ours is a partnership that has always been…and because of that I have always been blessed. Thank you!

Acknowledgments from Dave & Jon:

We want to acknowledge our parents, Earl and Pat Ferguson. Growing up in your house was a blessing. To have a mom and dad who continue to pray for us and always want to hear from us is a gift from God. The times around your table are still some of our favorite times in life. Thank you for serving us with your example and wisdom; but most of all, thank you for being the first to share the story of Jesus with us. Mom and Dad, you have truly blessed us!

Thanks to Mark Sweeney, our agent, for guiding our work and encouraging us along the way. Thanks to Lindy Lowry for helping to shape this book and offering editorial advice along the way. Thank you to Timothy Peterson, Karla Dial, and the other individuals who make up Salem Books!

Much thanks to Community Christian Church and NewThing for your belief in the vision of *"blessed to be a blessing"* and being willing to put these valuable practices into your daily rhythm to accomplish the

Jesus mission. It has been one of the great blessings of our lives to be able to lead you.

Thanks to the many people who shared their stories and expertise in blessing others. To name a few, Ian Simkins, Sharie Behnke, Jon Hughes, Kim Hammond, Rob Wegner, Daniel Im, Rick Richardson, Beth Seversen, Michelle Sanchez, Randy Frazee, Brian Bradford, Justin Ulmer, Lauren Seaman, and many more. Thank you!!

And finally, a deep and heartfelt thank you to our assistants, Pat Masek and Amber Stefanski. We never would have finished this book on time without all you do to help us do what we do. You two are a double blessing!!

But most of all, thank you, Jesus, for your example of how to B.L.E.S.S. our neighbors. We pray that you use this book to catalyze a movement that changes the world!

Dave Ferguson is the lead pastor of Community Christian Church, a multisite missional community that is passionate about "helping people find their way back to God." Community has grown from a few college friends to thousands and has been recognized as one of America's most influential churches. Dave also provides visionary leadership for the international church-planting movement NewThing and is chairman of the board and president of the Exponential Conference. He is an award-winning author of books that include *The Big Idea, Exponential, On the Verge, Finding Your Way Back to God, Starting Over*, and *Hero Maker*. Dave and his best friend Sue have three terrific children: Amy, Josh, and Caleb. Feel free to email him with questions, ideas, feedback, or introductions at daveferguson@communitychristian.org. Website: daveferguson.org. Twitter: @daveferguson. Instagram: @fergusondave.

Jon Ferguson is the co-founding pastor of Community Christian Church in Chicago, where he serves as one of its lead teaching pastors and provides leadership in new ventures. He helped co-launch NewThing, a church-planting movement that includes more than six thousand churches globally, as well as a movement of multiplying networks in the greater Chicago area. He also serves on the board of directors for the Exponential Conference and Thrivent Financial Chicago Region. He has co-authored *Finding Your Way Back to God, Starting Over, The Big Idea*, and *Exponential: How You and Your Friends Can Start a Missional Church Movement*. He resides in Chicago with his multi-talented wife, Lisa, and is the father of two wonderful children, Graham and Chloe. You can follow him on Twitter @jonferguson, on Facebook at facebook.com/jonferguson, on Instagram @jonferguson1, or on his website, www.jonferguson.org.

ENDNOTES

Chapter 1: Why Does Sharing Good News Feel So Bad?

1. "Almost Half of Christian Millennials Say Practicing Evangelism Is Wrong," Barna Research Group, February 5, 2019, https://www.barna.com/research/millennials-oppose-evangelism/, 5.
2. Ibid.
3. Zach Hrynowski, "How Many Americans Believe in God?" Gallup, November 8, 2019, https://news.gallup.com/poll/268205/americans-believe-god.aspx.
4. "Religion," Gallup, https://news.gallup.com/poll/1690/religion.aspx.
5. Rick Richardson, *You Found Me: New Research on How Unchurched Nones, Millennials, and Irreligious Are Surprisingly Open to Christian Faith* (Downers Grove, Illinois: InterVarsity Press, 2019), 59.
6. Barna Report, *Reviving Evangelism*, https://shop.barna.com/products/reviving-evangelism, 3.
7. Ibid., 4.
8. Ibid., 3.

Chapter 2: Could Simply B.L.E.S.S.ing People Really Work?

1. Madeleine L'Engle, *Walking on Water: Reflections on Faith and Art* (New York, New York: Crown Publishing Group, 2016), 199.

Chapter 3: B: Begin with Prayer

1. Beth Moore, *Further Still: A Collection of Poetry and Vignettes* (Nashville, Tennessee: B&H Books, 2004), 103.
2. Hudson Taylor, *Hudson Taylor's Choice Sayings: A Compilation from His Writings and Addresses* (London, United Kingdom: China Inland Mission, 2018), 61.

Chapter 4: L: Listen

1. David Augsburger, *Caring Enough to Hear and Be Heard: How to Hear and How to Be Heard in Equal Communication* (Grand Rapids, Michigan: Baker Publishing Group, 1982).
2. Rich Gorman, "Rich Gorman: Outreach from the Ground Up," *Outreach Magazine*, November 24, 2014, https://outreachmagazine.com/interviews/10777-rich-gorman-outreach-from-the-ground-up.html.
3. Dallas Willard, *The Spirit of the Disciplines: Understanding How God Changes Lives* (New York, New York: HarperOne, 1999), 210.

Chapter 5: E: Eat

1. N. T. Wright, *Simply Jesus: A New Vision of Who He Was, What He Did, and Why He Matters* (New York, New York: HarperOne, 2011), 180.
2. Henri Nouwen, *Bread for the Journey: A Daybook of Wisdom and Faith* (New York, New York: HarperOne, 2006), 294.
3. Alan Hirsch and Lance Ford, *Right Here, Right Now* (Grand Rapids, Michigan: Baker Books, 2011), 204.

Chapter 6: S: Serve

1. Solar Storms, "Lord Kelvin," SolarStorms.org, http://www.solarstorms.org/SKelvin.html.

Chapter 7: S: Story

1. D. T. Niles, *That They May Have Life* (New York, New York: Harper & Brothers, 1951), 96.
2. "Quotes from the Great Missionary St. Francis Xavier," Catholic Television, April 17, 2018, https://www.catholic-television.com/quotes-great-missionary-st-francis-xavier/.

Chapter 9: A B.L.E.S.S. Strategy for Changing the World

1. Dave Ferguson and Warren Bird, *Hero Maker* (Grand Rapids, Michigan: Zondervan, 2018).